SPARKS OF GLORY

SPARKS OF GLORY

by

MOSHE PRAGER

Translated by
MORDECAI SCHREIBER

SHENGOLD PUBLISHERS, INC.
New York

Library of Congress Catalog Card Number: 73-89415
ISBN 0-88400-000-1

Published by Shengold Publishers, Inc., New York
45 W. 45th St., New York, N.Y. 10036
in cooperation with
National Conference of Yeshiva Principals,
an affiliate of Torah Umesorah

INTRODUCTION

Amid the black clouds which billow out of the holocaust of European Jewry there are many flying sparks and flashes of human elevation. Who will gather them? On the bottom of the abyss, precious gems of Jewish courage are strewn about hidden from sight. Who will go down and retrieve them?

The following stories are such sparks of glory. They are holy sparks. They were picked with shaky hands from among the rubble and the ashes. They represent a modest attempt to bring together the scattered sparks which, joined, will burn as a mighty flame of *kiddush ha'shem,* the sanctification of the divine name.

These are not literary exercises. The language is not carefully groomed. The events recorded in the book are not imaginary. How can imagination compete with these harrowing events of our time? Just as our mind is too limited to fully comprehend the extent of the horrors, so is our sensitivity too dull and weak to grasp the full impact of the splendor which bursts out of the very darkness of death.

Against the somber backdrop of this horror-laden reality each spark stands out in all its shining glory. The new Amalek had attempted to erase the divine image from the face of mankind, and precisely at the time of the eclipse, as Satan, drunk with victories, was roaring with laughter, the Jew came along and once more taught the world the power of faith.

The words inscribed on this scroll are all witnesses. They were taken down directly from the heroes of the stories, who themselves did not realize they were heroes. These are true stories. They are all factual. They were all accurately recorded.

And if they appear to border on the miraculous, it is because they mirror an age of miracles. And if they make the soul tremble, it is because they are echoes of a terrible and lofty time.

These sparks of splendor were collected and kept, copied and passed on, with fear and with awe.

CONTENTS

Girl with the yellow badge in the Kovno Ghetto, by Esther Lurie.

Wooden bridge in the Kovno Ghetto, by Esther Lurie.

1

THE DANCE OF SUFFERING

THIS is a true story. It should have been recorded for all time in the age-old memoir of the venerated Jewish community of Lublin. This community, however, along with all the other communities of a once glorious Polish Jewry, was totally wiped off the face of the earth, and the memoir, together with all the other sacred books of Lublin, were reduced to ashes.

The time was the early days of the extermination campaign launched by the Nazi hordes against the Jews of Poland. The place was Lublin—a "mother city" in Israel. The original reporter of the events was the head of the community, who secretly passed the information along. Later some unknown person risked his life to record in accurate detail all the horrors committed by the enemy. This anonymous writer was fortunate enough to survive the war and to salvage what he had written. After he reached the shores of Israel, he hand-copied the entire record of events, down to the last detail. Since then the story has been kept in the nation's archives, to be retold from generation to generation, to be sung by future poets, and to be held up by future historians as an example of miraculous deeds,

Lublin was a city prominent in Jewish history; the seat of the Council of the Four Countries; the city which later became a center of Torah with the rebuilding of the illustrious Yeshiva of Lublin. It was this Lublin that was chosen, through some diabolic design, to be the first place for the Catastrophe to strike. It was there that the first detention camp, or *Reservat*, was erected. And it was there that the first transports of Jews, uprooted from their homes in Western Europe, were sent.

In the streets of Lublin the Germans staged an official public military ceremony, to the accompaniment of a full army band, for the burning of the books of the Great Yeshiva. And it was the Storm Troops' Commander Globochnik, a notoriously sadistic murderer, to whom the sad fate of the Jews of Lublin was entrusted.

The first thing this murderer did was appoint a time of assembly for all the Jews of the city. Young and old, men, women, and children were to come to an assigned place outside the city limits for a demonstration of torture and abuse. A decree was issued: any Jew who did not show up at the given hour would be shot. The frightened Jews considered the alternatives carefully. If they stayed at home, they would be doomed. If they went as ordered, they would be in grave danger, but at least there would be hope. They decided to go.

When the day came the Jews assembled promptly in great numbers. They stood fearful and trembling, prepared for the worst, but secretly praying for Divine intervention.

The assembly was held in an abandoned field on the outskirts of the city, completely surrounded by barbed wire. Armed guards stood everywhere, equipped for the occasion with whips in hand. The Jews stood trembling, their hearts quaking with mounting fear. What was the meaning of this grotesque show? What would the next moment bring?

The armed guards were ordered to form a double file. They were ready for something special to happen, for none other than Globochnik himself, the Commander-in-Chief, was personally overseeing the goings on. Globochnik, as they all knew, knew no bounds when it came to inventing ingenious tortures and clever tricks which he delighted to inflict on his Jewish victims. His troops, trained in brutality and bloodshed waited impatiently for the impending order.

The villainous oppressor was in high spirits. He was laughing uproariously, uncontrollably, without stop. His laughter curdled the blood of the hapless throng. He laughed and laughed as if the whole thing were nothing more than a joke. Even the orders he shouted sounded like nothing but a cruel jest.

"Sing, Jews!" He shouted. "Everyone of you will now sing! Sing, all of you together! Sing a happy song! Sing a Hasidic ditty! Do as I say, quickly!" he kept shrieking, and there was an ominous threat in his voice as he shouted his absurd order.

Sing? Is that all? Is that all the enemy wants? But how? How could these Jews in mortal fear for their lives suddenly burst into happy song? How could they bring themselves to sing a happy Hasidic song to these murderous barbarians?

The Jews remained silent. They could not open their mouths.

"Attack those stubborn Jews!" the commander blurted out, his voice now devoid of laughter. "Beat them with all your might!"

The armed guards followed the order, their ruthlessness matched only by their vehemence.

The Jews bit their tongues to hold back their cries, but could do nothing to stifle their sighs and groans.

"Push back those impudent Jews! Push them! Push them!" the enemy ordered again, shaking with blind fury. "Fast! Push them! Get going!"

The Jews were forced back against the barbed wire. The barbs pierced their flesh, pricking their bones, and the blood began to trickle and run. The Jews huddled and crowded together, stumbling and falling as more kept coming, colliding against the fallen ones and falling with them. Many were trampled under foot as each new wave of retreating people was pushed back.

In the midst of this confusion the shrieking voice of the murderous chief was heard again:

"Sing, arrogant Jews, sing! Sing or you will die! Gunners, aim your machine guns! Now listen, you dirty Jews. Sing or you will die!"

And at that horrifying moment, one man pried himself loose from the frightened mob and broke the conspiracy of total silence. He stood there all alone and began to sing. His song was a Hasidic folk song in which the Hasid poured out his soul before the Almighty:

"Lomir zich iberbeiten, iberbeiten, avinu shebashamayim,
Lomir zich iberbeiten, iberbeiten, iberbeiten—"
"Let us be reconciled, our Heavenly Father,
Let us be reconciled, let us make up—"

A spark of song was kindled, but that spark fell short of its mark. The Jews had been beaten, and recoiled. The voice of the singer did not reach them. His song was silenced. There was no singing.

But something did happen at that moment. A change took place. As soon as the solitary voice was hushed, humbly, another voice picked up the same tune, the same captivating Hasidic tune. Only the words were not the same. New words were being sung. One solitary person in the entire humiliated and downtrodden crowd had become the spokesman of all the Jews. This man had composed the new song on the spot, a song derived from the eternal wellspring of the nation. The melody was the same ancient Hasidic melody; but the words were conceived and distilled through the crucible of affliction:

"Mir velen zey iberleben, iberleben, avinu shebashama—yim,
Mir velen zey iberleben, iberleben, iberleben—"
"We shall outlive them, our Heavenly Father,
We shall outlive them, outlive them, outlive them—"

This time the song swept the entire crowd. The new refrain struck like lightning and jolted the multitude. Feet rose rhythmically, as if by themselves. The song heaved and swelled like a tidal wave, arms were joined, and soon all the frightened and despondent Jews were dancing.

As for the commander, at first he clapped his hands in great satisfaction, laughing derisively. "Ha, ha, ha, the Jews are singing and dancing! Ha ha, the Jews have been subdued!" But soon he grew puzzled and confused. What is going on? Is this how subdued people behave? Are they really oppressed and humiliated? They all seem to be fired up by this Hasidic dance, as if they have forgotten all pain, suffering, humiliation, and despair. They have even forgotten about the presence of the Nazi commander. . . .

"Stop, Jews! Stop immediately! Stop the singing and dancing!

Stop! Stop immediately!" the oppressor yelled out in a terrible voice, and for the first time his well-disciplined subordinates saw him at a loss, not knowing what to do next.

"Stop! Stop! Stop at once!" the Commander in Chief pleaded with his soldiers in a croaking voice.

The Jews, singing and dancing ecstatically, were swept by the flood of their emotions and danced on and on. They paid a high price for it. They were brutally beaten for their strange behavior. But their singing and dancing did not stop.

2

THE STORY OF A SIMPLE JEW

I stood there and listened with bated breath to the innocent words of that Jew, who unfolded before me the saga of his sufferings in his journey through seven Nazi concentration camps. Unwittingly, the question escaped from my lips:

"And were there Jews who prayed in that hell?"

"What a question! Even I prayed every single day."

"And did you have *Tefilin* there, in the death camps?"

"Of course. I put on *Tefilin* and I guarded them in all the camps and under all conditions.

"How? How can one believe this? And those monsters, what did they say?"

"What's the difference? Nothing can stand in the way of man's will."

The words were spoken in utter simplicity. The man did not raise his voice. He did not stress any words, as if he had no idea that he was talking about something truly lofty and exalted.

"I had made a vow not to let a day go by in the camp without putting on *Tefilin*. It was not easy to keep the vow. The obstacles were multiplied every day. It was difficult to guard the *Tefilin*, to keep them from falling into the murderers' hands. It was doubly difficult to find time each day for prayer—even for only a moment of prayer—which our enemies might not notice. After all, they kept watch over us day and night. And yet I managed to pray. For man is led in the way in which he chooses to go. And I was not the only one, Heaven forbid. In every camp Jews joined in the prayer. We knew that the punishment for such a crime was death. But what did it matter? Our life was worthless anyway. Each of us knew that his fate was sealed. So what did it matter how it happened? Better yet, a death by a guard's bullet was much easier than all the other kinds of gruesome deaths in the extermination camps. I knew I was going to perish with all the others, probably of hunger or from illness, like so many thousands of others. I thought to myself: If this is the case, isn't it better to die for the crime of praying, or putting of *Tefilin*? So I kept my vow . . ."

"What a miracle! Were you ever caught?"

"What's the difference? Of course I was caught. More than once. But I managed to escape. One time they announced a curfew inside the barracks. We all knew that anyone who dared cross the barracks' door during the curfew would be shot on the spot. It was late. Time for *Mincha* prayer. And I hadn't yet put on *Tefilin*. The *Tefilin* happened to be in the barracks across the way. They belonged to another Jew who like myself had made it his point to pray every day. It didn't take me long to sneak out of my barracks and into my neighbor's. I put on the *Tefilin* and said a short prayer. I took them off and started out on my way back. I was caught this time. The head of the block had noticed me. He was a Pole, a convicted criminal, whom the Nazis had appointed as our tormentor, and who outdid them in brutality. I knew that this time I was lost. The criminal wanted to know what I had done and why I had risked my life. I thought to myself: this is it. This is the end. I told him I had to go out to pray because my *Tefilin* were hidden somewhere outside.

"What he subsequently did I can't understand to this day. He burst out into wild laughter and howled:

"'Don't lie to me, you despicable *Jid!*' And suddenly he ordered me to bare my arm and show him the marks of the *"Pachorki,"* the Polish word for *Tefilin*. I showed him my left arm, on which the marks of the hastily bound straps were clearly visible.

"'You spoke the truth, you *Jid!*' Again he burst into wild

15

laughter, and I was sure my end had come. With this he went over to the alarm bell nearby and summoned all the inmates to a quick gathering. When all the inmates gathered, shaking with the fear of impending doom, that gentile criminal began his speech:

"'All of you who have gathered here are lowly and despicable dogs! I would have never believed that there was still one person left among you who was willing to die for his faith. I have just found him, and there he is, standing before you! From this day on he is permitted to pray openly, and whoever dares stop him from praying will be risking his life!'

"I couldn't believe my ears. I thought perhaps it was Elijah the Prophet who had appeared under the guise of a brutal foe. . . . It was a real miracle, as indeed all those assembled considered it to be."

"And since then you were never trapped again?"

"Here is what happened once. In one of the camps I chose an open pit, which had been dug for the burial of the dead, as my place of prayer. Because of this the Jews called the pit the "Little Synagogue." During the short rest period allotted to us while we were doing hard labor in the field, I jumped into the pit and prayed. And sure enough, there I was caught. A German murderer pulled me out as I was wearing my *Tefilin*. He knocked me down to the ground, and stepped on me with his iron studded boots, grinding his boot in my stomach while peeling the skin off my face with his other boot. I lay on the ground and I knew I would never get up again."

"And what did you think to yourself then?" I asked.

"What's the difference what I thought? I don't know . . ."

It was obvious that he was suffering under the barrage of my questions, reliving the past with each answer, but hardening my heart, I urged him on. It was precisely this hidden spot in his soul that I wished to uncover.

"All right, I will tell you the whole truth," he said, "As I was writhing in pain and felt all my powers ebbing, I recalled a verse from the Book of Psalms: 'See my suffering and my ordeal and forgive all my sins—' I repeated this verse over and over again, and it may be that because of it I was able to rise up—and go on with my prayers . . ."

16

3

A SECRET PRAYER IN THE BASEMENT

BRAVE little Shmulik was known throughout the ghetto for his resourcefulness. At a time when fear followed every Jew like a dismal shadow, Shmulik was unafraid. The high wall and barbed wire around the ghetto represented no barrier for him. The armed guards who would shoot to kill were no deterrent. Shmulik went on about his business.

Of course, it helped that the guards were as stupid as they were cruel, and that Shmulik was as crafty as he was quick. Squatting motionless, close to the ground, Shmulik, swathed in his rags, looked like a heap of garbage. But suddenly the garbage heap was halfway up the wall, clinging to the barbed wire with bruised fingers. And before the fat, goose-like German soldier could turn his rotund body toward the climbing boy—Shmulik would have scaled the wall and disappeared on the other side.

There was one time, though, when Shmulik did get caught. But not by the fat German soldier. Shmulik made his heroic leap over the wall only to be met by a Polish policeman who had been waiting for him, whip in hand. The bitter sting of the leather thong on his back was something Shmulik could not quickly forget.

One Friday afternoon Shmulik recalled how on Fridays the farmers from the neighboring villages would come to the weekly fair in the market place. It was not the kind of fair that was held in the old days, since the Jews were locked up behind the walls and all the bargaining took place among *goyim*. Still, it was worth a try. . . . Shmulik could well remember the farmer who used to come to his father's house. His father was a shoemaker in the village and used to mend the farmers' boots. . . . Yes, it was worth a try. Perhaps he would find something in honor of the holy Sabbath. An onion, a carrot, a raddish, some grits or a handful of beans. Perhaps he would get lucky and find some potatoes. Certainly not a sack of potatoes, like in the old days. The peasants had learned how to take advantage of the hunger pangs in the Ghetto. They now counted every potato, as one would count gold coins.

Luck smiled on Shmulik and he was indeed able to acquire a great deal of potatoes. All of his pockets and the lining of his clothes were filled with them. His mother cried with excitement when she saw the great treasure and kept murmuring "In honor of the holy Sabbath, in honor of the holy Sabbath." His father, absently, began to hum a Sabbath song: "This day is honored above all days, this day is honored . . ." Shmulik, aching from head to foot, did not want to mar their joy and did not tell his parents how he had paid for those potatoes with his own flesh and blood.

Shmulik writhed in pain, tossing in his bed from side to side, his head spinning. He saw the policeman's coarse face before him, and again he felt the whip on his back. . . . To this day he had never felt fear. True, his life was in constant danger. Each day brought its casualties. The Germans kept shooting and killing. Some of his friends had been shot dead, but that, after all, was life in the ghetto! Each day a race took place between himself and the German bullets. He was prepared to accept the fate of being shot. Was he any better than his fallen friends? But the pain, the pain inflicted on his sunken body by the policeman's whip was driving him crazy. The pain scorched him, burning incessantly like a red hot spit stuck deeply in his flesh. He would have liked to cry out to ease some of the hellish pain. To cry out, to let some of the heat pent up inside him escape. But how could he, Shmulik, yell and cry in front of Papa and Mama and dim the joy of the approaching

Sabbath? Shmulik bit his lips, while in his heart he shouted without a sound: "I won't give in, I won't tell anything. I won't."

Now, on the morning of the holy Sabbath, when the spirit of the Sabbath filled the room and the odor of mother's cooking permeated the air Shmulik kept his pain to himself. Father, who had gotten up early in honor of the Sabbath, took a deep breath inhaling the stew's fragrance and rejoiced: "Ha! It will be a truly enjoyable Sabbath!" And mother, reading her *Tzenah U'r'enah*, stopped reading and purred, "Our Shmulik, our Shmulik."

But the thought of the whip, the nagging thought of that whip which does not kill or maim but merely makes the entire body burn, this thought burst out of Shmulik's tightly shut mouth: "Father, tell me Father, why the whip, the whip . . ." Shmulik's words were cut short. He had almost revealed his secret by his question, giving in to his pain. At once he overcame his weakness, and the words got stuck in his throat. By the time his father came in to see what happened, Shmulik managed to change his wording.

"Father, Father, why do the *goyim* beat us up?"

"Because we are Jews," his father answered in a loud, emphatic voice, as if he had been prepared for the question all along.

"And how do we get the strength to endure all this?" Shmulik insisted, seeking an explanation for his pain.

"By being Jews!" his father answered as loudly and emphatically as before.

"And is it worth it, Father? It is really worth it?" The question, painful and bitter, escaped from Shmulik's lips, as if against his own wishes and in a voice not his.

"It's worth it, it's worth it, Shmulik, my son. Because we are Jews!" Father's voice became soft and pleading. "Enough now, my dear boy. I will explain everything, but right now I am in a hurry. It's the Sabbath. I must go, I must go . . ."

"Where are you going, Father? And why are you going? Why? Why?" Shmulik inquired tearfully, and he felt he had many questions to ask, and the questions were greatly relieving his pain and putting out the fire in his bones.

"Why am I going? Because I am a Jew!" Father's answer was curt as he hastened to leave.

"I understand, Father. You are going to pray. I would like to

19

go, too. I would also like to pray!" Shmulik jumped out of bed as if he had just found the antidote for his pain.

"Shmulik, please. Be a brave boy. Not today! Perhaps next Sabbath. The enemy discovered our secret place of prayer and we had to find another place. We swore not to take any children along. We will pray without the children. Children sing too loud during the service. And of course it is not mandatory for children to pray with the congregation. You children should be spared if we adults are caught . . ."

"Father, Father, I want so badly to pray today with all the Jews. Especially today!" Shmulik called out, wailing. But his father had by now slipped out of the room and left. Father walked along looking around as he walked with fear and suspicion. He was going to pray at the risk of his life. . . .

The place was a basement inside a basement. A dark, damp, musty basement like all other basements, except that one wall was hung with a red velvet curtain embroidered in glittering gold. Behind the curtain in a deep hole in the basement wall was a single Torah Scroll, salvaged from the impure hands of the enemy. This scroll kept drawing the sorrowful Jews, hungry for solace and inspiration. The velvet curtain caressed them, soothing their pitiful stares. The golden embroidery glittered in the dark, kindling sparks of hope in their sunken, extinguished, despairing eyes. Very quietly, the Jews congregated. Very quietly they prayed, a silent prayer, a prayer from the depths. The death trap of the demon of destruction was spread all around them. The demon had boasted of being able to separate the beaten Jews from their Heavenly Father. A decree had come forth from the oppressor, deeming public worship a serious crime, punishable by death. These Jews, at the risk of their lives, has joined together in prayer. The prayer was subdued, an outpouring of the heart, saturated with choking tears which were unable to escape. More than a prayer, it was a silent cry of anguish. A cry purged in the crucible of suffering, consuming the soul. The prayer released the oppressive pain, burst through the locked gates, pierced the heavens and rose up to the Throne of Glory.

His father had left, and Shmulik was left burning with inner pain, his heart throbbing and bursting with his unrelieved anguish,

20

and all his senses drew him to the secret path, leading to the wondrous healing fountain. . . .

A strong knock shook the basement door. A daring, nervous, tremulous knock. A knock different from the agreed secret knock.

A shudder ran through the entire congregation. The prayer stopped and breathing also seemed to stop. The knocking continued, becoming more insistent, more determined. A dark fear descended upon the crowd of worshipers: they have found us! The end has come! But soon a change of mood took place: we are ready to die for the sanctification of the Holy Name. Come what may, we may just as well get caught in the act of committing the crime of praying. And if we are to die, let there at least be some purpose and reason for our death.

The congregation was now prepared for any foreseeable calamity. One man walked over and opened the heavy door when lo and behold . . . little Shmulik was standing meekly at the open door, knocking on the gates of prayer.

A wave of relief swept the crowd at the sight of the frail figure, relief followed by a rush of outrage. Shmulik's father pushed his way through the congregants in the basement, his face livid with anger. "Such chutzpah, Shmulik," he yelled in a voice not his own. "Who are you to disobey orders?" and he delivered a slap across his son's face—a painful, humiliating slap.

Shmulik could no longer contain himself. The physical pain compounded by mental anguish were too much to endure, and Shmulik allowed himself the luxury of tears.

"Will you beat me, too?" he cried. "Haven't I had my share of blows? I, too, am a Jew. I, too, want to pray . . ."

4

A STRAY PAGE FROM THE BOOK OF PRAYER

THEY sat there for a long time without uttering a word. Each man was absorbed in the stirring events of his own past, listening to the musings of his heart. One man, nicknamed Siberiak, no longer able to contain his pent up emotions, began to talk. At first he spoke in a hushed, muffled voice, as if speaking to himself, but as he grew more vehement his voice intensified and his friends began to listen. What they heard sounded like a sequel to what he had just been whispering to himself.

"The question remains: Is there anything in the world that is truly real, absolutely essential, recognized by all people as having great value, absolute value? What is it? I know, someone may say, gold. Another may say, bread. Or some such thing. But I, Siberiak, after having been through the strangest twists and turns of fate, I have my own opinion on this matter. An altogether different opinion. Both gold and bread are of questionable value, and there are things which are worth more than both of them put together.

"Gold, which all mortals worship, is only a delusion. If your luck had taken you to a gold mine, as mine did, you would have been ready and willing to exchange a pound of pure gold for a dry morsel of bread. And even bread itself, on which man depends for his survival, is not of absolute value.

"Precisely at a time of a great famine you may completely forget your hunger for bread and feel a spiritual hunger, which, if satisfied, will sustain you physically."

The total conviction with which he spoke surprised the listeners and prompted the entire group to come closer and listen. He paused and introduced himself: "Siberiak is the name." Someone wanted to know where he had gotten such a name. Was he a native of that frozen wilderness which made one feel the icy breath of eternal snow by the mere mention of its name? Perish the thought. Fate had taken him to Siberia. Jewish fate had driven him beyond the mountains of darkness to the cold and ruthless regions of ice and frost. While Satan was unleashing his fury upon the Jews of Europe and burning them alive, this man's luck permitted him to exchange the fiery furnace for Siberia's frozen steppes.

Lucky man . . .

Siberiak came to the point of his story:

"When that big sleigh, harnessed to half-a-dozen gigantic Siberian dogs, brought us to the end of the world—somewhere near the Sea of Ice, I was in a holiday mood. Just as well, I said to myself. The further from the dark clouds of the Nazi holocaust the better. But the next day and in the days that followed my stomach began to rumble, and the question 'What to eat?' became more and more unsettling.

"I said before I was a lucky man. There are many kinds of harsh and cruel labor out there in Siberia. That whole country is nothing but oppression and slavery, one giant labor camp for life prisoners. Nature itself is cruel to men in Siberia, and men are cruel to one another. The task masters, who oversee the hard labor, are themselves condemned people without any hope of becoming free again. So they pour all their anger and fury upon the heads of the newly arrived prisoners. There is no lowlier form of slavery than to be a slave to slaves . . . but, to make a long story short, my luck took me directly into a gold mine.

"There I was, surrounded by gold. Real gold! Glittering gold. Living gold. Untouched by human hand. Gold! Gold! The dust under my feet was gold. The stream coming out of the bowels of the mountain contained gold. The stone walls of those wild mountains, strange and enormous, striking fear in man's heart, were threaded through with veins of gold. And all that gold belonged to me! It was all mine! You look puzzled. Well, whose was it if not mine? No one had laid any claim on it. No one owned it. It was a natural resource. First come, first served. It belonged to whoever bothered to dig it up, wash it, and caress it with trembling hands. What a miracle! What a miracle! I was taken to Siberia in chains. I was a prisoner. And suddenly the chains came off. My hands were let loose to do hard labor and here I was inside a gold mine, free to do as I chose. I became a gold digger. Certainly not a shameful occupation. It was not easy work, but it was clean work. I stood all day knee-deep in the stream gushing out of the mountain and sifted grains of sand swept by the stream. I was uncovering gold ores. . . . Sometimes I would sift the finest dust—gold dust. Sometimes I would find grains of gold or even gold nuggets. Shapeless, oddly formed nuggets—yet nuggets of gold all the same! Could it be true? I was drunk. I had gold fever. I was burning with it. I became delirious. All my senses were on fire. . . . The whole world was drowning in blood and mire and here I was amassing gold. . . .

"I was very puzzled at first: why was my guard so negligent in keeping a watch over me? At sundown I would drag my frozen bones to the blazing iron furnace inside the large cabin in order to dry and warm myself a bit. I would go through the inspection, amazed at how careless it was. I would hand over the basket with the gold which I had collected, and they would take it without saying a word. How I rejoiced when they didn't search me! I had succumbed to the gold fever. I kept a bottle full of pure gold. My gold. My gold treasure kept growing every day. Was I robbing anyone? The gold was free for all. Anyone could take it. Even the guards didn't pay any attention to it. Obviously I was not committing any crime. . . . And so the gold kept intoxicating me, feeding my fantasies in the daytime and my dreams at night. Gold . . . gold. . . .

"But the rude awakening was not long in coming. This happy dream of gold was a vain dream. It disappeared suddenly, without any trace. One clear day I threw away all my gold. I despised it. It was a false treasure, an empty illusion, a hoax. Does it amaze you to hear me say so? I could no longer stand my hunger and I went searching for food. I thought to myself, 'Now I will never have to go hungry again.' After all, I now owned a gold treasure. But when I mentioned it to those wretched slaves who had been working for years in the gold mines, they laughed and heaped insults upon me. I offered them gold for bread, and with derision more bitter than death they replied, 'What is the worth of gold compared to the worth of bread? Bread is life. Bread is warmth. Bread is a friend. Gold is a trap. Gold is madness. Gold is emptiness and desolation.' I now realized why the taskmaster were so lax in watching me. Why they had put the gold treasures of the mine at my disposal. I threw away the gold which I had hoarded. And after I freed myself from the Moloch of gold, I became aware for the first time of the bitter seed of separation which that Moloch had been planting in our hearts. Since the day I was first hit by the madness of gold I became a lone wolf who shunned human company. A mere look would scare me. Every person I met was plotting to steal my gold. On the long and torturous journey to Siberia we Jewish prisoners had become as close to one another as brothers in trouble. We had all shared a common fate. And here came the curse of gold and separated us. Each of us was worried and concerned only about his own gold. Each had his own golden shell to protect him from the rest.

"No sooner did I free myself from the tyranny of gold than I became enslaved to a new tyrant called bread. I pursued the very shadow of bread—yet there was none to be found. There was gold everywhere, but as for bread—not even as much as an ear or even a grain of corn. You could try any trick imaginable and still find no bread. You were surrounded by a sea of snow and by virgin forests capped with eternal ice that stretched out of sight. If you got lucky you might have found a wild mushroom. You kept your priceless find where no one could see it—it was your only food! You went out and scavenged in the garbage dumps, hoping to find at least a piece of paper, for even paper was a substitute for bread. You could roll it into a cigarette. A burning cigarette might at times be even better than bread. It made you forget your hunger for a moment, causing reality to disappear, bringing instead distant, foggy dreams.

"And if any of you may ask: A cigarette made up of a dirty, torn, worn out piece of paper, what good is it, when all it does is emit some rancid, suffocating smoke? Then let me tell you: Siberia! We are talking about faraway Siberia, where there are no printing presses and where even the art of writing is superfluous. Man lives a simple life out there, and has no use for the blessings of technology. Husky dogs and polar bears provide him with abundant meat and skins for his sustenance and clothing. The absence of what we call paper does not bother him, so he lives out his days without it. One of our kind who happens to wind up in Siberia would trade his gold and even his bread for a piece of paper which could blow smoke in his nostrils and fill his brain with a cloud of dreams, following the philosophy of 'Let him drink and forget his sorrow.'

"Still, all hope for finding paper in Siberia was not lost. Twice a year the mail would be delivered. First in the dead of winter, by a special sledge on the icy trail. Then, during the short summer, after the thaw, by a steam ship on the river. I got lucky. It was winter. The Siberian cold reached its lowest mark. The bells were announcing the great event of the mail arrival. . . .

"Everyone in the camp knew that many snow-tested Siberian boys served in special units fighting in the snowy mountains, and thanks to them a piece of paper might find its way to Siberia, their distant homeland. A letter or an envelope or a piece of paper. During those days of mail delivery I went hunting after a piece of paper, and my search was crowned with success. A rich peasant living near our camp had a son out in the front. That son, having been taught in the army how to read and write, hastened to let his parents know he was alive, which was how that peasant happened to get a letter. The peasant, not knowing how to decipher the mystery of the dark marks, came to me, the learned Jew, for help. My reward came unexpectedly. The letter came in an envelope. The peasant listened to the cipher of the tiny markings in the letter, and in his great excitement, he threw down the envelope, which now became my prized possession. I was rewarded with an unusually thick piece of paper which could be used for some truly enjoyable smoke! Fortunately, the nagging peasant went away, leaving me the great treasure. I ran back to camp. I wanted to hide from human eyes so that I wouldn't have to share my prize with

26

any of my fellow prisoners. Heaven forgive me! I didn't do it out of selfishness. I had no choice. If I had invited all those people to stand in line for a whiff of smoke, quarrelling and fighting would have broken out among them. So I hid in my corner and began to lose myself in the rare pleasure of rolling a cigarette when. . . . It couldn't be! I saw black letters printed on the inside of the envelope, square Hebrew letters!! Not any ordinary letters, either. These were holy letters from a book of prayer! It was a page torn out of a *siddur* which had mysteriously found its way to Siberia. . . .

"Jewish prayer books, torn and defiled, were probably scattered through the streets of Europe along with Jewish corpses. This gentile soldier, a native of Siberia fighting in the distant front, must have used the torn pages of a Jewish prayer book for many of his needs. One of those pages now fell into my hands, and I was determined to save it from further desecration. That driven leaf out of the prayer book was making a changed person out of me. I was ruffled and perturbed and all the Jews who began to find out about it were equally affected. It was good tidings from an antediluvian world, from a world which had disappeared without a trace. Now the contact was established. The sign was given. The memory was reawakened. . . .

"I held the half-torn page in my trembling hands, and I said to myself that I was not worthy of keeping such an exalted and sanctified treasure. I decided to hand over this holy pledge to one of the Jewish prisoners, the one we called 'Rebbe'le,' a nickname both respectful and derisive. That prisoner knew how to determine the dates of the holidays and festival. None of us knew how 'Rebbe'le' did his calculations. We were simple Jews and we did not pay much attention to those matters. Our 'Rebbe'le' played with the dates of the holidays all alone, figuring the joyous festivals and the Days of Awe.

"Now came our Rebbe'le's great moment. I made the announcement to him about the discovery of the holy object. Tears of joy welled up in his eyes and with great devotion he kissed the torn page. I entrusted it to him and from that moment on the Rebbe'le's importance grew immeasurably. He would be seen carrying our holy treasure wrapped up in a bundle upon his heart and like a beacon of light which attracts the wayward, this treasure would draw all the Jewish prisoners from all the camps that surrounded ours. Who had spread the word about it? It was a miracle which had no explanation. From time to time some stray, hidden, self-effacing, forgotten Jew would bare his soul before the Rebbe'le. We all knew that from now on we were no longer isolated and forsaken souls without any hope or purpose. We were no longer cut off and separated from our Jewish roots. We now had a sacred and timeless find. And this holy possession infused a new spirit into us, rekindled a new, long-forgotten hope in our hearts, the hope that we may yet live to see the day of our deliverance from this Siberian hell.

"That torn page from the book of prayer had great mysterious virtues. If any of our men had to take an oath during a dispute, he would do it by holding the page. Whoever was seized by despair and didn't have the stamina to go on would kiss the saved treasure and would instantly regain his strength. Whoever was nearly frozen to death would have the page placed under his head and would then recover.

"And that 'Rebbe'le,' who now became the guardian of our treasure, would not allow a Sabbath or a holiday slip by. With the help of our page he would summon all the Jews to prayer. We all came. It was a short prayer. Our entire prayer consisted of what was on that single page. Each time a different person would read what was printed on both sides of the paper. At times I was the *sh'liach tzibur* for that service, and I remember exactly what was written: the last verses from 'Then Sang Moses,' the entire *Yishtabach* prayer, the *barechu* with the beginning of 'He Who makes light upon the earth,' to the verse 'Lord of the Universe in Your great mercy have mercy upon us.' That short prayer was truly remarkable. We all prayed enthusiastically, willingly, and in holy fervor. And when the prayer ended we felt a warmth and true enjoyment. What could that icy, cruel, deadly Siberian jail do to the outpouring of the Jewish heart engaged in prayer?"

The Siberiak concluded:

"That driven leaf from the book of prayer provided us with warmth until the day of our deliverance from the Siberian land of ice."

5

THE JEW AND THE TORAH

AN eternal covenant exists between the Jew and the Torah. Ever since Sinai the two have been joined together, bound by a common fate. Yet at no other time in the history of our people has this bond of common fate between the Jew and the Torah been more pronounced and more deeply felt than in our own, when the cursed beast arose before our very eyes and plotted to wipe the Jews from the face of the earth.

Let us evoke a few stories from the annals of the Holocaust, and tell of some Jews who fought for the honor of the Torah, and who, in that same act, fought for their own honor as well as for the honor of the entire nation.

a. Saving Torah Scrolls from Burning Synagogues

The first thing the Germans did when they entered a Jewish community in Europe was to set fire to the local synagogue. The purpose of this act was to terrorize and demoralize the Jews. It was done openly, in broad daylight, sometimes to the accompaniment of a German army band. On occasions the enemy would gather the local Jews and force them to watch the destruction. Using the latest weapons, German troops would fiercely assault the House of Prayer —the Jews' bastion of strength. More than once, though, someone among the oppressed and persecuted Jews would defy death and rush forth in holy fervor to rescue the scrolls of the Torah.

❖   ❖   ❖

In the community of Pshevorsk, Poland, both the Synagogue and the House of Study were engulfed in flames. Hordes of German soldiers and officers stood there enjoying the spectacle. Many Jews were gathered behind them, their heads bowed in pain and humiliation. The rabbi of the community had been ordered to stand in the front row, himself an object of scorn and derision. But suddenly the rabbi torn away and began to run. Two more Jews were seen running after him. The Germans stopped laughing and shouted after him to halt. But the rabbi did not hear a thing. Nothing could stop him, not even the flames. He and the other two disappeared inside the burning building. The Germans were speechless with astonishment. A few moments later the rabbi reappeared. His clothes were singed, but his face shone with a triumphant smile, as his two hands held a scroll of the Torah.

"Jewish impudence!" the German commander grumbled, accompanied by the rest of his men. They pointed their rifles at the burning synagogue, so that the two men who assisted the rabbi would not be able to come out. They attacked the rabbi with the butts of their rifles, but the rabbi held onto the Torah as if he and the scroll were one and inseparable, as, in fact, they were . . .

❖   ❖   ❖

In the community of Breslau, Lower Silesia, Germany, a special technical company of the Nazi Storm Troops, the S.S., was busy blowing up the synagogue. The blast of the explosions shook the entire neighborhood both physically and morally. The roof of the synagogue was blown to smithereens, and the whole building was reduced to a heap of rubble. The enemy had finished his assignment and had posted guards to make sure no Jew would come near the debris. Nonetheless, Jewish boys came by stealthily and searched in the ruins for fragments of Torah parchment.

They succeeded, at the risk of their lives, in rescuing almost an entire Torah scroll which they managed to extricate from the debris in several pieces. Only a few years later their vindication was complete when they were able to bring the torn segments to their old-new homeland, Israel, where they were able to replace the missing parts. There, in Israel, those boys, now adults, celebrated the completion of the scroll of the Torah. It was a celebration of their victory over their inhuman tormentors, whose ignominious end had by then arrived.

b. With a Torah in Hand on the Last Road

Jews and their Torah scrolls were as attached to one another as a flame to a candle. You could not separate them without extinguishing the light, and whatever happened to the Jews happened to the Torah. The Germans would rob the Jews of their last possessions, and when the Jews hid their remaining belongings, they also hid the last scrolls of the Law.

When the noose of death tightened around them, the remnants of the Jews would take their scrolls underground, into basements, caves and bunkers. To preserve them, they would put the scrolls inside tin cans or wrap them in tarred paper. When they were taken out of their hiding places to perish in the death camps, many Jewish leaders were seen marching on their last road holding a scroll of the Law.

❂ ❂ ❂

In the community of Tchernowitz, Rumania, the order of total evacuation astounded the Jewish population. Within a few days all the Jews in the city were forced to leave their houses and all their possessions and assemble on the road. The confusion among them was great, and the fear of the unknown was even greater. Young and old, women and children, babes in arms, the sick and those near death, all were huddled together. Behind them was their home town, the only home they had ever known and loved. Before them—a road shrouded in fear and desolation.

Suddenly the white bearded rabbis appeared, holding the scrolls of the Torah with all the silver regalia. They proceeded calmly and peacefully, holding the scrolls on high, as if in a joyous celebration. This splendid sight calmed and soothed the multitude. There was neither cowardly nor hysterical behavior, and the armed guards who accompanied the crowd were denied their amusement. Imbued with a sense of dignity the Jews set out on their last journey.

❂ ❂ ✳

A few remnants of Jews, chosen by fate, the last Jews of Europe, were gathered in the camp of detention, Vital, France. They came from Poland and France, from Belgium and Holland. Among them

31

were rabbis and writers, delicate women and frightened children who had been through all the spheres of the Nazi hell. These Jews had cards showing them to be nationals of American countries. The German murderers were not quite sure what to do with them, but the bitter day finally came, and the order was issued to deport them "Eastward," that is to say, to Poland, to the death camps.

The lot was cast. Among those deported were famous rabbis, including the rabbi of the Jewish community of Antwerp, Belgium. The aging leader marched toward the death train. He was the last in line. He marched briskly with an uplifted head. Even the murderers looked on in surprise. With one hand he led a small boy whom he had miraculously rescued during a manhunt in his community. On his other arm he held a scroll of Torah. The train began to move. Inside the train sat the old rabbi firm in his faith, with all that remained of a great Jewish community: a child on one side of him and the Torah on the other.

c. Jewish Partisans Avenge the Desecration of Torah Scrolls

The German murderers fought not only against the Jewish people but also against their spirit and their teachings which animated and influenced human history. That is why the murderers made it their point to defile every Torah scroll on which they were able to get their hands. They made floor mats out of the Torah covers. They made shoe soles out of the parchment. But they paid for it more than once. The Jewish Partisans who avenged Jewish blood also avenged Jewish honor. They would salvage Torah scrolls from the hands of the unholy and would mete out measure for measure.

❖ ❖ ❖

In the last phase of the liquidation of the *Wilno Ghetto, the "Jerusalem of Lithuania,"* the German command ordered to wipe out every remnant of Jewish life and spirit. They launched a hunt for Jews to be brought to the slaughter houses. At the same time they wrought their fury upon the Torah scrolls. A great number of the scrolls was gathered in the Ghetto and transferred to a German shoe factory. When the Partisans went into action against the German foe they saw to it that not only Jewish life but also Jewish spiritual treasures were saved from annihilation.

❖ ❖ ❖

The Jewish Partisans took control of the forests, in the areas of Polesia in Eastern Poland. Squads of fighting Jewish Partisans terrorized the German murderers and their Ukrainian and Belorussian minions in the surrounding countryside. When a unit of Jewish Partisans went into action in the villages, it would make sure to discover those who assisted the Germans and who took part in the murder of the innocent.

In one cottage a Jewish Partisan found a strange carpet. He checked the carpet and a shiver ran through his bones—it was the desecrated cover of a Torah scroll. The partisans did not believe the peasant's explanations and set fire to the cottage.

They told the peasant to announce that anyone who was found to have desecrated the holy objects of the Jews or to have touched the Jews themselves would live to regret it.

d. Remnants of Torah Scrolls Saved from Destruction:

After the German defeat, hidden Torah scrolls were discovered throughout Europe just as hidden Jewish children were discovered. In the liberated city of Lodz a widely attended public funeral was held for shreds of Torah scrolls, which were buried in a common grave, and its impact was similar to the one made by a funeral of the bones of Jewish martyrs.

In Munich, the capital of German evil and depravity, the Jewish soldiers found in a basement ancient and invaluable Torah scrolls, which the enemy collected for "research" purposes. The soldiers purged the scrolls and distributed them among houses of prayer which were set up for Jewish survivors.

In one community in Italy the Jewish remnants renovated a synagogue which had been desecrated by the Germans. To the inauguration of the synagogue came a local Christian carrying a Torah which he had salvaged by hiding it in his church.

And somewhere in Europe, amid the salvaged remnants of Israel, a Torah scribe who survived the holocaust is probably sitting down, dipping his quill in his inkwell and trying it on the parchment, beginning anew the task of writing a Torah scroll: "In the beginning—"

For the Jew is eternal and the Torah is eternal, and the two, the People of the Book and the Book of Books are bound together forever.

6

A SONG OUT OF THE DEPTHS

WHERE does a tune emerge from in a time of trouble? Does it descend from a pure, distant heaven? Or does it burst out of the bowels of the earth, out of a wellspring in the great deep?

The Jewish tune is the language of the soul. It is the echo of the bitter and desperate struggle with the earthly, wingless body. The tune is an upward flight to the heights, a rebellion against matter, an aspiration for the sublime. The notes of the tune touch and awaken hidden chords in the soul of the nation. And the melody grows, drop by drop, like a spring of pure, crystal tears. Each sigh of pain, each quiver of hope, each rumble of anger, each whisper of joy, each yearning of the soul is stored up in its depths.

This then, is the secret power of the tune.

Many generations put their noblest hopes and dreams into the tune. And in time of darkness, in time of great trouble, the tune comes to the rescue. It liberates, and it redeems.

The eruption of the tune is wholly miraculous. All around is destruction, horror, and bereavement. A destructive flood obliterates everything in sight. Yet that same flood also arouses the upsurging fountains of the soul, conjoining them into a mighty stream of song.

The melody plays on the subtle strings of hope. It has the power to soar higher and higher upon the wings of endless devotion. It seethes with bitter derision. It has the power to burst in the face of the enemy with the eternal notes of Jewish confidence, and also to accept the Judgment while yearning with one's last breath to die for the Sanctification of the Name.

❀ ❀ ❀

Always, in times of trouble, the tune will emerge.

A group of Jews imprisoned in a Nazi Concentration Camp, nearly starved to death, was marching in file to do forced labor. Their faltering legs refused to carry them on. Pharaoh, who was the first to enslave the Jews in ancient times, caused them to cry out from hard work, but they were not denied bread or even meat. Here, however, they were begrudged even a morsel of dry bread. The goal here was to break their will, destroy their spirit, divest them of all dignity, and make them crawl in the dirt. The task-master's whips kept slashing through the air: *Schneller, Jude Schneller!* (Faster, Jew, Faster.) The tormentors' cries of contempt reverberated rhythmically and incessantly, and the Jews mocked those cries with a bitter melody. They answered with ridicule and with aversion, word for word. The oppressors' contempt met with open derision. The derisive melody became a marching song. The Jews' steps livened up, their backs straightened, and they vigorously sang their tune, imitating the cries of the wicked:

> Faster, Jews, Faster,
> Faster, Jews, Faster,
> Faster, faster, faster.

❀ ❀ ❀

When the Jews were put into the Lodz Ghetto, isolated from the others by the order of the Nazis, one of them was appointed as the "Elder of the Jews." The others, derisively, nicknamed him "Pauper King." The "Pauper King" oppressed and persecuted his fellows. He would ape the "royal" manners of the Germans. Just as they barked orders, so would he. Just as they would cast terror around themselves, so would he. This "Pauper King" who would bow down to the shadow of the least and lowliest of the enemy, would demand regal honors from his fellow sufferers, the prisoners of the ghetto. And the humiliation of the downtrodden Jews was as great as their suffering.

Along came the ghetto minstrel, Yankele, and with the help of a satiric couplet he was able to lift up the spirit of the opressed and the persecuted. In all parts of the ghetto the satiric song was heard:

> Hayyim, oh Hayyim, a "Pauper King,"
> Let us this good man's praises sing,
> Scraps he throws to us, like a friend,
> While he eats our flesh without an end.

*　　*　　*

In Rumania, which surrendered to the Nazis, the murderers did not bother to build gas chambers and ovens, nor did they use bullets. The extermination campaign was simple: All Jews, young and old, men and women, were driven out of their homes and away from their native grounds, and were taken on a march of famine through desolated and scorched land. The exiles died of either exhaustion on the way, or of hunger in the exiles' camps. Many of them began to feel that quick death by a bullet might be better than death by starvation. And what was it that gave them some small cheer? What brought some solace to their ebbing souls? The Song!

Who invented the hymn of the famished? An unknown, ordinary Jew. But his song captivated every heart, strengthened every knee and brought a smile to the yellowing faces of the starved:

> Stomach, oh stomach, why do you rumble?
> You are neither a princess nor a duchess.
> Yesterday I gave you everything I had,
> Today I can't give you more than I have.

*　　*　　*

The enemy said: "The ghetto is a proper living space for the Jews. When the Jews live next door to non-Jews they poison the world. But in the ghetto, without any strangers among them, let them do whatever their hearts desire." But the enemy's malice went even farther. The Jews were shut within the ghetto walls, and in the narrow streets armed soldiers moved about and checked every corner. The teaching of Torah to Jewish children had been strictly forbidden, and any Jew caught in this criminal act faced the penalty of death.

In the holy Community of Cracow, the city of the RaMa and the BaH and the great men of the Torah of every generation, the students of Torah went underground into deep bunkers. Above them, on the surface of the ghetto prison, ruled the accursed enemy. But beneath the surface, in basements and underground tunnels, ruled the chant of the Gemarah. The students of Torah sat together in clusters. Old men with long white beards, studying Torah for its own sake; young yeshiva students trying their skill in the stormy sea of the Talmud; and children, who found a special taste in the clandestine study of the Torah, a pleasant and flavorful taste. They were all woven together in the tapestry of the soft and sad chant rising from the Gemorah: Oy, oy, said Abaye, oy, oy the sages taught!

One of the men in the crowd of students recalled the horrible reality outside the bunker, and his chant was heard rising above the rest, a catchy chant in which the others joined:

> Oy, oy, were it not for Your Torah my delight,
> Oy, oy, Your Torah my delight,
> I would be lost, oy, oy, oy,
> Were it not, were it not, Your Torah, oy, oy.

❖   ❖   ❖

Who can describe the suffering of children who, not having yet known the taste of life, were growing up in the shadow of death and destruction? The only right to life in the ghetto was the "work card." The Jewish children who were the first ones to be sent away to their death understood by natural instinct what fate awaited them, and so they flocked to the places of work. They tried to pass for adults. They put on adults clothes, wore shoes with high heels, and used all sorts of tricks to appear older. The children strained to work long hours, doing backbreaking jobs and even outdoing the adults, to prove their efficiency and their worth.

In moments of despair the children would derive comfort from the perennial fountain of song. And here is the song which was composed by a group of children doing forced labor:

> We sing a sad song,
> About the troubles of the Jews,
> About our sorry condition.
> We are still children
> But we have learned how to suffer,
> How to bear and suffer, bear and suffer.

* * *

The Hungarians learned from their Nazi masters how to buttress their battalions by having groups of Jewish slaves trail behind the combatants at the front. Those groups were the first ones to become victimized by all the disasters of war. When the Hungarian troops launched an attack they would send out the Jews to pave the way by attracting the enemy's fire to themselves. When the troops retreated, they left the Jews behind to be decimated by the advancing troops.

And so the beaten and downtrodden Jews would suffer from the victories as well as from the defeats of the oppressor's army. In their hopeless plight, the only relief they had was singing. Their singing was marked by soul-searching and the yearning for reconciliation with their Heavenly Father.

One member of the doomed group began singing his supplicating prayer, and all the rest joined in:

> Master of the Universe, Lord of the World,
> Behold our plight, empty of hope.
> We will return to You with our whole heart,
> Do not delay our redemption, please do not delay.
> Fulfill the promise of all the prophets,
> And let all people say, the Lord He is God.

* * *

There were dozens of races and nationalities in the Russian Army. They spoke in many different tongues. And yet the Jewish soldiers, many of whom had been raised among the gentiles and came from different countries and different cultures, sought one

38

another out and stuck together. Others also drew together, united by their common hatred for the Nazi enemy. But the Jews were different from all the others, and there was something holy in their hatred. It was a hatred for Amalek tempered by a trembling, sorrowful, deep-running Jewish wrath.

Many songs of vengeance were sung by the troops of the Red Army, songs of hate in all tongues and dialects. But the special tune of the Jewish soldiers was an ancient Hebrew chant permeated with the fury of the Biblical Reproof:

> All the curses in the Reproof—
> On your heads, accursed beasts,
> All the curses in the Reproof—
> In the Reproof.

❀   ❀   ❀

The Holy Yeshiva of Slobodka, one of the strongholds of Torah and piety in Europe, had just been captured by the enemy. The young students of the yeshiva were taken away along with their illustrious and famed rabbis. All was known. The path was known. The purpose was known. It happened on the holy Sabbath. They were all caught in the midst of prayer. The march proceeded without any excitement, with almost spiritual exaltation. They had reached the highest rung of self sacrifice—supreme satisfaction in fulfilling their mission. No hesitation. No inner struggle. No questioning. The march continued in quiet and solemnity. As they marched they continued the Sabbath prayer, following it to the letter: "The breath of every living being shall bless—as it is written 'All my bones shall proclaim, O Lord, who is like You—.'"

The march continued to the sound of the chant of the holy Sabbath prayer. It was the last road they would tread . . . the melody was soft and restrained. The inner melody engulfed the marchers and let them to the place of sacrifice:

> By the lips of the upright You will be praised,
> By the words of the righteous You will be blessed,
> By the tongue of the faithful You will be extolled,
> And in the midst of the holy You will be sanctified.

❀   ❀   ❀

A fiery, relentless thirst for fighting and vengeance.

Rivers and springs of Jewish blood flowed everywhere in broad daylight, screaming out for revenge. The Jewish Partisans, ruled by a fiery, relentless thirst for fighting and vengeance were unconcerned with saving their own skin. Day and night they sought revenge as they defied danger and death. They were a living testimony to the spiritual valiance of the Jew. They were a living proof of what the Jews could have done had they been given weapons to defend themselves.

These dauntless warriors, the fighters of the ghetto and the avengers of the spilled blood of Israel, proved by their battle hymn that they were Jews. Their valor was not drawn out of poisoned wells of hopeless despair, but rather out of the eternal wellspring of Israel's faith and hope:

> Oh never say this road you're on is your last way,
> The longed for day will yet arrive as you may pray,
> And with its light the clouds will surely clear away.
> The light of dawn will mark the new day's birth,
> As our foes and sorrows will have vanished from the earth.

7

ROSH HASHANA IN THE BESIEGED CITY

THE year 5700 is engraved on the Hebrew Calendar of Horrors as a black year; a year darker than 4856, when the fanatic Crusaders left a trail of Jewish blood in their wake; a year more horrible than 5408-5409, when Chmelnitzki and his Cossack hordes massacred the Jews of Poland, leaving death and destruction behind them. For on Rosh Hashana, 5700, the Holocaust began, and the Nazi demon cast his fury upon Warsaw, a "mother city" of European Jewry.

At twilight on the eve of that awful day the German troops surrounded the Polish capital with a noose of fire. Squadrons of bombers above and batteries of guns below kept firing incessantly, sowing death and destruction. Yet in every basement and in every bomb shelter where there were Jews, a stirring call made the rounds:

"Jews, the Holy Day is coming! It is time for prayer!"

The streets were blocked. All sorts of barriers were strewn everywhere. The sidewalks were broken up. Everywhere there were ditches and trenches—traps for the enemy's armor. Each house was a closed and fortified battlement. And each of these battlements that housed Jewish residents became a private house of worship as well, where Rosh Hashana services were held.

But at dusk, as the prayers were commencing, the shelter dwellers were shaken by the sound of the alarm siren which pierced the air.

The people's ears had become impervious to the sound of the siren. They had been hearing it day and night. Its sound had mingled with the sounds of the explosions and no one paid any attention. But this time, at twilight, at the time of the ushering in of the new year, the siren had intensified its scream and kept wailing on and on.

The city burned.

The enemy kept dropping thousands of incendiary bombs and the flames rose like mountains of fire. Clouds of fire billowed, entering shelters and basements and suffocating the inhabitants.

The equanimity of the Jews under siege began to waver. It became clear that there was no escape from this storming, spreading conflagration. Even the deepest shelter was not safe. The flames and the suffocating smoke penetrated holes and cracks, consuming everything along the way. In their panic people began to leave their shelters and their hiding places. But when they stood outside, under the open sky, they were nonplused: There was no way out! The entire Jewish quarter of Warsaw was burning!

That night Jewish Warsaw was no longer a besieged city. Everyone poured out into the streets. Everything had become a free for all. No one heeded the bombing and the shelling. Death lay in wait in every hidden corner and in every shelter in the ground as it did in the open streets. No one bothered to black out the windows. It was a needless precaution, for all of Jewish Warsaw was lit up by the flames. A sea of light had set it aglow.

And amidst all that light, new darkness and gloom descended, as the bad tidings began to spread as rapidly as the all-consuming fire.

"Dozens of Jewish houses are collapsing with their residents inside! The houses hit by bombs are caving in and the tenants who did not have time to escape—are being burned alive!"

Thousands of Jews, residents of once glorious Warsaw, found their graves in their homes, and the frames of the buildings looked like blazing torches in the netherworld, or like huge memorial candles on fresh graves. . . .

In the midst of the pandemonium a cry suddenly pierced through the horror-laden air:

"Jews, do not linger! Come to prayer! Come to the Rosh Hashana service."

It was a lofty and terrible prayer! A prayer which soared through the seven heavens. A prayer which rent the curtain separating Israel from their Heavenly Father.

In the courtyards of raging death, amid the pillars of fire, smoke, and soot, amid the falling walls of the collapsing buildings, the Jews huddled together shaken and perplexed, and poured out their hearts before the One Who dwells on high:

"Put Your fear O Lord our God upon all Your works and Your awe upon all Your creations, and let all Your works be fearful of You and all Your creatures will bow down before You—

"And all wickedness will vanish like smoke, and the reign of evil will be gone from the earth—"

8

THE ONLY ETROG FROM THE LAND OF ISRAEL

IT was the Eve of Sukkot, 5700, in Nazi occupied Warsaw.

For nearly a month the Polish capital had held out against the tidal waves of armored Nazi Storm Troops until it finally collapsed and fell, and the crooked cross appeared above its ruins.

When the news of the surrender became known, the people of Warsaw, schooled in suffering, came out of their holes after hiding in them for a month. Their ears, accustomed to the roar of guns, were astounded by the heavy silence which had descended upon the city. Gone were the terrifying sounds of diving bombers and thundering guns; a deep suspicious silence followed the fearful storm, a silence which belied the horror of destruction wrought by the storm.

In the streets of the city, on piles of smouldering debris, people reunited at last with their loved ones, were seen embracing and kissing one another with tears of joy in their eyes.

"Are you still alive?!"

"You survived too?!"

Others, less fortunate, lamented their dead.

"Why go on living? My wife and my children were buried alive under the wreckage!"

44

"Why live? My only child perished in the fire in his mother's arms!"

Still others reacted with a joyous cry of survival:

"Hurrah! If this angel of death didn't get me this time, he never will."

"I saw death a hundred and one times and I was saved!"

In this commotion of joyous shouts and anguished cries a warm and soothing call was heard:

"Our brethren, sons of Israel, tonight is the eve of Sukkot! Let's hurry up and build a sukka, the holiday is almost here!"

Never in the history of Warsaw, since the day the city was founded, was there such an abundance of boards and beams for the building of festival booths as on that day. Lumber in all shapes and sizes—the remnants of destroyed buildings, cluttered the roads and the alleys.

As the Jews attached board to beam to fulfill the commandment of building a sukka, a question troubled their minds:

"And what about a permanent abode? The debris of steel and cement bear silent witness to the destruction of stone houses, which can no longer provide even a temporary shelter!"

But he who is engaged in fulfilling a commandment has no worries . . . so the people who were busy with the commandment forgot about their worries concerning permanent lodging. They joined board to pole and pole to beam, up came the walls, the thatching was put on top, and a beautiful sukka was erected!

At noon that same day the booths stood in the courtyards of the Jews. In the evening, when the blackout ordinance was ended, candlelight flickered through the sparse thatching in honor of the festival.

The next day, at sunrise, the question began to worry those Jews who were concerned with the precise compliance with the Law:

"What about the commandment of the four species?"

The Torah says: "And you shall take on the first day the fruit of citron trees, fronds of date palms, boughs of myrtle trees and willows of the brook." Now that they were fortunate enough to remain alive, was it possible that they would let the holiday go by without saying the blessing over the Lulav?

It was early morning and the Nazis had not yet set foot into the conquered city. They were determined to enter the capital in a spectacular victory march. Meanwhile the thirsty residents began to roam the streets looking for water. During the siege the water reservoirs in the city had been bombed and a water shortage hastened the surrender. When our Jewish brethren went out with the rest of the people to look for water they heard a rumor which quickly took wing:

"There is an etrog in the city! One solitary etrog in the entire city of Warsaw, and not any ordinary etrog either, but one of the best!"

The rumor was verified.

In the last plane from Palestine which reached Poland a few days before the war broke out, an etrog, or citron, which was mailed to one of the leaders of the Jewish Community, a certain Reb Meshulam, arrived. Both the etrog and its owner were fortunate enough to survive the Nazi invasion, and so Reb Meshulam availed himself of some myrtle and willow, which were picked at the bank of the Visla by a Jew who had risked his life to venture out of the ghetto. Luckily, a lulav which remained from the previous year was discovered, and the Four Species were complete.

When the Jews found out that there was an etrog in Reb Meshulam's house, they hastened there to say *Shehecheyanu*. The throngs besieged the house and a long line of Jews was formed, waiting to fulfill the commandment of "And you shall take for yourselves . . ."

He who did not see that line of some ten thousand Jews, waiting in fear and trembling before Reb Meshulam's house, never saw Jewish throngs anxious to fulfill a commandment!

In one place in the Jewish quarter, where Djelna and Pavia Streets meet, two lines also met. One was a line for water, stretching back to Zamenhoff Street, to the well in the jail house which was not damaged in the siege and supplied water in abundance. The other was a line winding through several streets, longer than the first. Those in the second line waited to enter the house on Eleven Pavia Street—where the etrog from the land of Israel was.

Each line had its own character. On the water line stood men with all kinds of vessels in their hands: pails, jars, pots, basins, kettles, tubs, and the like. On the opposite line stood men with empty hands and glowing faces, a holy fire burning in their eyes as they stood festive and proud. Among them were great rabbis and teachers, old Hasidim and young men in their holiday clothes, common, "everyday" Jews, who did not have time to change their clothes in honor of the occasion. Many of those who stood on the water line holding their containers began to switch to the other line; they too were seized by the fervor of fulfilling the commandment. The bodiy thirst for water was forgotten, replaced by a spiritual thirst for fulfilling the commandment.

The etrog line kept growing, kept getting longer. In the big library on the second floor Reb Meshulam stood and urged the pressing crowd:

"Hurry up, hurry up! Jews are waiting in line!"

The etrog from the Land of Israel, spreading its aroma, was passed from hand to hand. The Jews said the blessing, shook the lulav and left. And if one of the blessers would linger a little longer with the etrog in his hand out of love for the commandment, having finished the blessing, Reb Meshulam's impartial words would be heard:

"Move on! Move on! Thousands of Jews are waiting in line! They all want to fulfill the mitzvah!"

9

THE FEAST OF FREEDOM OF THE ENSLAVED

PESACH, Festival of Unleavened Bread, the Season of our Liberation. How painful was that aspect of the Festival of Spring to the hapless victims of the Nazi bondage; victims who felt the daily sting of the whip upon their backs in the ghettos and labor camps. "We were slaves unto Pharaoh," it was written. It would have been more accurate to say "we *are* slaves."

And yet, the spirit of this people who had known trials and tribulations since the time of Abraham could not be broken. The Festival of Freedom knocked on the gates of the ghetto, and the people enslaved inside responded to its call by cherishing every token and symbol of the holiday, even at the risk of their very lives.

* * *

When Pesach drew near, one worry filled the ghetto: Where would we get matzos for the Holiday?

The ghetto, locked and barred as it was, was a horrible prison for all those held captive in its midst. These unfortunates were at the mercy of the Nazi oppressors. The Angel of Death reaped his harvest with the help of his two emissaries: hunger and disease. But when Pesach approached, the ghetto woke up from its lethargy of despair:

"Passover, the Season of our Deliverance, has come!"

"What has Passover to do with us?" one of the gloomy Jews sighed. "After all, we are enslaved by the wicked enemy . . ."

"Heaven forbid! We are not slaves!" another one rejoined. "Anyone who does not accept the life of bondage, anyone who aspires and believes in and even fights for freedom in every possible way, is a free man! We believe in freedom and we will fight our oppressors, so let us celebrate the Festival of our Freedom!"

"We'll even bake matzos for the holiday!" the prisoners of the ghetto decided. But since the enemy's eye was forever open and watchful, the baking of matzos had to be brought underground. This dangerous operation was headed by some pious Jews who were willing to risk their lives in order to fulfill the commandment of eating matzo on Pesach. They were joined by some dauntless young men.

The operation was successful. An oven was prepared in a secret place, supervised by a rabbi. The problem of procuring flour was left to the young men. How they managed to get the flour, how they smuggled it into the ghetto—these were things no one asked and no one offered to tell. The men were tight lipped, and the job got done.

In the dead of night, on the night of the Fourteenth of Nisan, the night before Pesach, a *minyan* of Jews gathered at the bakery. Everything was arranged hastily, as in the story of the Exodus from Egypt. They, too, "could not tarry," for danger lurked on every side. The chores of baking were quickly distributed. Some prepared the dough, others rolled it out to wafer thinness, still others marked the holes in the matzos, and the rabbi supervised the sacred work as his lips moved quietly:

"For the sake of the mitzvah of matzo, hurry up, Jews. For the sake of the mitzvah . . ."

They worked with great haste. The fastest of all was the matzo remover—the one who inserted his shovel into the oven and brought out the steaming matzos. His face was flushed as he glowed with inner joy. From the depths of his soul a tune emerged. The tune flowed and soon flooded the bakery. It was the ancient song of the Hallel:

"When Israel came out of Egypt, when Israel came out, came out, came out—"

And the tune carried with it all the Jews who were busy with the baking of the matzos. It grew louder and louder, imbuing the singers with a sense of the freedom of which it told. But suddenly the singing stopped, shattered by the noise of shouting and yelling.

"*Donnerwetter! Zum Teufel! Verfluchte Juden! Kreuzdonnerwetter!*" (Dammit! to the devil! Damned Jews!)

The door opened, and a German Storm Trooper in polished uniform appeared in the doorway.

"What is this? What are you doing in here, you despicable Jews?"

The Jews were dumbfounded. They couldn't utter a sound.

"Why are you so quiet all of a sudden, you cowards?"

The matzo remover who had started the song was the first to respond:

"Tomorrow is Passover. We are baking matzos for the holiday!" His voice was loud and unhesitating.

"Arrogance! Jewish arrogance!" the German commander shouted. "How dare you celebrate your holidays before our very eyes! You will pay for this with your life!"

"That Jew," the commander pointed at the matzo remover, "get rid of him. Wait! Don't waste a bullet! Beat him! Beat them all!"

The order was carried out, and they were all beaten mercilessly. The matzo remover was cudgeled to death. His head was smashed with the heavy roller which the Jews had used for rolling out the matzos.

But the Seder was observed as planned. At dawn the Jewish children gathered the crumbs of the broken matzos which had soaked up the martyred blood. And in the evening the crumbs were put on the Seder table as a sign that this time the commandment was sanctified by the martyrdom of the matzo remover.

"This is our Paschal Sacrifice," the prisoners of the ghetto said. "This is the Paschal Sacrifice of the ghetto!"

❀   ❀   ❀

According to the slave laws applied to the Jews in the concentration camp, boys and girls over 12 were compelled to do hard labor.

Some five hundred Jewish girls were interned in a labor camp for girls in Upper Silesia. The supervision of the camp was entrusted to the "S.S. Women," or female Storm Troopers. Those Nazi women underwent special training, and their savagery exceeded that of their male fellows. They literally worked the weak Jewish girls to death. They starved them, they robbed them of all they had, they took off their clothes and shoes and tortured them endlessly.

There was one girl in the camp who came from a family of pious Hasidim and who brought a prayer book along with her. Her father had given it to her when she was taken away. All the Jewish holidays were recorded in tiny letters on the first page.

The girl guarded that Siddur like the apple of her eye. In time of great trouble, when the oppression became unbearable, she would read some Psalms from the Siddur to her girl friends. She would read those Pslams which spoke about the wicked with special emphasis, foretelling that they will be "like hay blown in the wind," that "the wicked will return to damnation," and that "they will be caught in the net which they had put out," and then both she and her friends would feel relieved. More than once, when despair overwhelmed them all, the girl would check the calendar of the holidays in her Siddur, and then proceed to calculate and find out when the next holiday would be coming. She would then look for some way to celebrate that holiday without getting caught.

One day the owner of the Siddur announced that Pesach was only a few days away. "Let's hold a secret Seder on the eve of Pesach, like the Marrano Jews used to do in Spain," one of the girls said. "I once read a story about it . . ."

"I have an idea," another girl said, excitedly. "We will put a white sheet on the table, and I will give you all the candles I have left to light in honor of the holidays."

"In my Siddur I have the entire Haggada of Passover," the owner of the Siddur said brightly. "We'll read together all the stories of the Exodus from Egypt."

"But the table will be completely empty without any Passover food," one girl sighed. "If we could only have one matzo to remind us of the holiday."

"No matter, we will celebrate the Seder," said the owner of the Siddur, and she added, in a whisper, as if praying, "Perhaps a miracle will happen and we will have a matzo for Pesach after all."

And the miracle did happen.

Not far from the labor camp there was another large camp. It housed French prisoners of war. When the girls went out to work in the fields of the surrounding villages they could see the prisoners, dressed in army uniforms. The Nazis' treatment of the Frenchmen was infinitely better than their treatment of the girls. The prisoners were neither beaten up nor wantonly tortured. But the girls knew that the prisoners were forbidden to come into contact with any Jews.

One day the girls met a group of prisoners marching back to camp singing, and one girl noticed how one of the prisoners dropped a folded piece of paper. She furtively picked it up and brought it with her to the camp. The paper read as follows:

"My dear Jewish girls: I am a Jew just like you. This is a secret which the enemy mustn't discover under any circumstances. I am among the prisoners. I'll help you in every way I can. Let me know what you need. Please leave a note under the square stone outside the gate. Do not despair, girls. Don't lose hope!"

The man did not disclose his name, but the girls knew that they had come across a sympathetic Jewish heart and they decided to accept his kind offer.

In their reply the girls asked the anonymous prisoner for some white flour for the baking of matzos. Early in the morning, when they went out to work, they placed the note under the stone. The next day, when they returned from work, they noticed a package which was tossed over the barbed wire fence. In the package they found a small bag of flour, with a note attached to it:

"Congratulations, my dear girls! I envy you, for you know how to observe our holidays. I am proud of you. I got the flour from a fellow prisoner, a Jew like myself who gets packages from home. I share your joy of the holiday with all my heart. I hope to get you some candy for the holiday. Be strong and of good courage!"

In the middle of the night a few girls got up and went to work They posted guards at the entrance and at the windows. They took apart a bench and fed the wood into the large furnace in the main hall. They used bottles as rollers to flatten the dough, and before long, having surmounted all obstacles, each girl had wrapped a few hot, tasty matzos in her kerchief. The girl who owned the Siddur said,

"This is not ordinary matzo. This is *Matzo Shemurah,*" guarded matzo, for we have guarded it from all foes and destroyers!"

❖　　❖　　❖

Men often fear the beasts of the forest. But during the Nazi era the most dangerous beasts lurked *outside* of the forest's limits.

Within the forest the Russian Partisans were sole lords and masters. Beyond its edge, the Nazi animal lay in wait. Thus the Jews knew that while certain death awaited them outside the forest, inside its bounds they were protected. It was for this reason that the

52

Jewish Partisans hurriedly brought every Jew, young or old, whom they could salvage from the clutches of the Nazi beast, into the safety of the forest.

In this way many Jews came to this wooded refuge. Among them was an old Jew who had rescued a scroll of the Torah, which he guarded zealously and never let go of.

Living conditions in the forest were extremely precarious. Since no food could be found locally, everything had to be brought in from the outside. Packages were dropped from Russian war planes, but these, more often than not, contained weapons and ammunition rather than foodstuffs. The only other source of supplies open to the Partisans was the local Nazi-controlled villages, which served as supply depots for the German troops. These were raided often by the Lords of the Forest, with relative success.

With their bounty, the Partisans were able to feed and maintain their various "guests." And in return, the survivors would do their best to help the Partisans. The old Jew who never let go of the Torah scroll showed his gratitude by arranging a place of prayer for the Partisans in a rustic cottage. His stirring prayers and blessings which saw the Partisans off to battle touched the hearts of the Jewish warriors, and they bestowed upon the old man the title of "Rabbi of the Partisans."

"I am no rabbi," the old man objected. "I was the sexton of a synagogue which was burned down by the Germans. When they started the fire I ran in and rescued a Torah scroll. Heaven be praised, I have been able to preserve it intact to this day."

The Partisans would come and pray at the little cottage. When a Partisan had a *yahrzeit* for a father or a mother who had been murdered by the Nazis, they would hold a public prayer. The Partisan would say *Kaddish* and would swear by the Torah to avenge the blood of all the murdered Jews. And the old man, the "Rabbi" of the Partisans, would say with great devotion,

"Amen, amen!"

After the thaw, when the first signs of spring appeared in the forest and ushered the coming of Pesach, the Rabbi of the Partisans spoke to his visitors whom he loved like his own children:

"Listen, my dear ones. I depend on you all year for my sustenance. Please, for this coming Pesach, get me some wheat so that I may grind some flour which is ritually fit for baking matzos!"

The Partisans undertook to fulfill the old man's request. In one of the raids on the villages they confiscated a large store of wheat, a good portion of which they set aside for the baking of matzos. The old man prepared a special hand mill, and with the help of the Partisans built a special oven in accordance with the strictest traditional specifications of Pesach.

"The most important thing, my dear children, is that all of you come to our Seder." The old man repeated his invitation every chance he had. "No excuses, please. Do come."

"We will all come," the Partisans promised, "We are also the children of Abraham, Isaac and Jacob. We want to celebrate Pesach like all Jews everywhere."

It was not an easy promise for the Partisans to keep. When spring arrived the fighting between the Partisans and the German troops was renewed with great intensity. Movement in the forests became easier and the Partisan units launched extremely daring attacks. The Nazi troops were forced to resort to more drastic methods and every now and then they tried to venture into the forest. These daring attempts on the part of the Nazis presented new opportunities for attracting the enemy into various traps and dealing him severe blows. The forest hummed with activity and the Partisans' hands were full. Nevertheless they remembered Pesach and the promise they had made to the old man.

"We ask for a short leave, comrade commander," a group of Jewish soldiers told the head of the fighting camp on the eve of the holiday.

"It's hard to grant your request at this time, comrades," the commander stood firm. "The time is too crucial, and no one can leave his post."

"But we have a holiday tonight. We have promised to participate in the Holiday of Freedom, and we shouldn't break our Partisan promise." The Jewish Partisans were equally insistent.

"What holiday? What's this talk about freedom? Are you playing a joke on me?" the guard asked, obviously angry.

"We are Jews. Today Jews all over the world celebrate the liberation from Egypt. We have been celebrating this holiday for thousands of years."

"Oh Jews, Jews! You always make trouble. You always give me headaches," said the commander, suppressing his anger. "Ah, well, get out of here quickly, only make sure to do guard duty at dawn!"

The Partisans left humiliated and with heavy hearts. They hastened to their destination, the quiet Jewish corner inside the forest, but they couldn't get over their pain. It was the first time their commander addressed them as *Zid.* . . .

"Welcome, welcome, my dear children! O happy holiday to you and to all Israel!" the old Jew shouted joyously when the Partisans arrived at the cottage.

"Happy holiday, happy holiday!" the Partisans replied as they were greeted by the festive spirit in the cottage. A table was set, laden with matzos, with candles aglow in the center. But most important was the presence of a group of children; those few children who were miraculously saved.

"Why are you late, my friends?" the old man complained. "I have waited for you impatiently. I couldn't start the Seder without you!"

The Partisans poured out their hearts before him. True, they got permission to get away, but at what price. . . .

The old man, instead of consoling them, began reciting the Haggada of Pesach:

"This year we are here, next year may we be in the Land of Israel, this year we are slaves, next year may we be free men . . ."

And the old man added his own commentary:

"I want you to know, beloved children of Israel, that this has always been our fate here in Exile. Here we are slaves, and only there, in the Land of Israel, can a Jew look upon himself as a free man!"

"It is true," the Partisans agreed. We have told ourselves more than once that at least here among our comrades in arms we won't know the taste of Exile, but we have learned our lesson."

"*Lebedig, Juden, Lustig, fröhlich* (rejoice and be merry, Jews)," the old man cheered up his guests, and gradually they joined in the circle of joy, until the trees shook from the sound of the singing which broke out of the shabby cottage.

"Next year in Jerusalem!" the old man concluded the reading of the Haggadah. "Without it, Jews, we have neither holiday nor freedom! Next year in Jerusalem!"

And the Partisans responded in a mighty voice,

"Amen, amen!"

10

SEDER NIGHT IN PRISON

THE men sat together, crowded and bent, in the large prison room. It was a common ward for Jews and Poles who were locked up for diverse and unusual reasons. Among the prisoners was an aging Rosh Yeshiva, caught by the Germans teaching Torah to his students in a secret basement. One of the prisoners sitting near the old rabbi was a cantankerous apostate, an ex-Jew who was a former high government official. The Germans had stamped the word *Jude* in red ink on his I.D. card, and made him wear a ten centimeter wide arm band with a yellow star. During an inspection the arm band was found to be too narrow and the ex-Jew found himself in jail.

Among the prisoners were some young men and even children. Some were caught climbing the ghetto walls trying to escape. Others were imprisoned for hiding small bags of food inside their ragged clothing—food like groats, flour, and sugar, which was deemed "too good" for Jewish consumption. Still others were jailed for being caught with the most objectionable wares of all—propaganda fliers and underground newspapers.

Among the prisoners were many Jewish peasants who had no

idea just what their crimes were. Some were thrown into the prison for being out in the street during curfew. Others, for not showing proper respect to the Germans. But most of them were jailed merely because of a suspicion that they *might* do something which could harm the German conquerors.

In that dull, harsh dungeon everything had a dingy gray cast about it, as well as an aura of timelessness. It was almost impossible to distinguish between day and night, and it was forever dark in the low ceilinged hall. There were neither days of work nor days of rest, but rather each day brought with it its own torture. The only way to note the passage of time was by the arrival of the guards who came in to take one of the prisoners on his last ominous walk.

One day the entire jail room was aroused. Through the high narrow window penetrated a pale ray of light. Whether it was the light of the sun shining somewhere in the outside world, whether it was a moon beam, no one could tell for sure. But, at that uncertain moment, the voice of the aging Rosh Yeshiva was heard as he called out,—*Gut Yontef, Jews!* Why are you so quiet? Today is Pesach! It's the first Seder night!

All the prisoners, including the Poles, had treated the Rosh Yeshiva with respect. They all regarded him as an extraordinary person. He, the Rosh Yeshiva, knew the reckoning of the Sabbaths and the weekdays, and even of day and night, and he would pray quietly, morning, afternoon, and evening. At the time of even the most terrible tortures he would draw joy from his hidden, inner wellspring. This time he apparently sought to share his joy with all the Jews in the jail.

Some derisive remarks were heard in the crowd:

"Nu . . . nu . . . a seder yet!"

"On the contrary, let him set up a Seder *here!*"

"Nu . . . And four cups of wine? Or at least one sip . . ."

"Hee, hee, hee, and matzoballs, rabbi . . ."

"And a piece of matzoh, if only for remembrance . . ."

The Rosh Yeshiva did not seem to hear them:

"My dear brothers, Jews! The Haggada I know by heart. The 'Ma Nishtana' we won't ask because we have nothing here to prompt the questioning. But what does it say in the beginning of the Haggada? —'This year we are here, next year may we be in the Land

57

of Israel! This year we are slaves, next year may we be free men!'
Do you hear? We Jews, we are not slaves! A man is only a slave
if he admits it, and we do not admit it! Next year free men, Jews!"
The Jewish prisoners, old and young, religious and free-thinking,
began to gather around the old Rosh Yeshiva who had stirred them
up, infusing them with hope for deliverance. At one corner of the
room a "Seder table" was set up. The Jews sat around it on straw
filled bags. Even the apostate came over stealthily and joined the
crowd. There was no sign of the holiday, not even a single solitary
candle, only the festive voice of the Rosh Yeshiva reciting the story
of the Exodus.

"We were slaves unto Pharaoh in Egypt . . ." the voice flooded
the room. The old man recited the words of the Haggada and the
entire assemblage repeated them after him, as if they had all been
transported to an enchanted world.

Suddenly the chanting stopped. The Polish prisoners seemed to
have been startled by the strange scene in front of their eyes. Some
of them jumped up from their seats, madly furious:

'That's Jewish impudence for you! *Bojnitza** You are making
here?!"

The Jews did not even have time to answer them and calm
their spirits, when some inmates started kicking the cell door and
whistling to alert the German guards in the hallway.

The head of the guards, a Storm Trooper, came in with a few
soldiers, a riding crop in hand.

"Damned Jews!" he snapped, foaming at the mouth. "You can
stil think of praying and singing! Incredible! *Kreuzdonnerwetter
nocheinmal!* To the gallows I will take all of you, tomorrow!"

And he turned to the loudest of the Polish prisoners and said
to him:

"You will keep an eye on them! I hereby appoint you as supervisor over all the inmates. I don't have any time or patience for
them right now. But tomorrow I will let them have it. And you,
Talmud *Jude*," he turned to the old man, "You will be the first one!"
And he slammed the cell door behind him.

An oppressive, painful silence ensued, lingering on for a long

---

*Synagogue

time. Both Jews and Poles felt totally helpless. No one knew what to say, and even the chief organizer of the raucus did not feel at ease in his new role. "Woe to him." It was the voice of the Rosh Yeshiva that broke the silence, soft and tremulous, as if it were not meant to be heard. "Woe, woe to him who of his own free will becomes a slave to the wicked. Woe, woe . . ." and as he spoke the Rosh Yeshiva began sobbing quietly, without stop. The crying, it was obvious was not so much the result of suffering as of deeply felt compassion. It was followed by muffled sobs which emanated from a good number of bitter souls.

"Shame on you, hiring yourself out to the henchman!" One of the tight lipped young men suddenly stood up and faced the new "supervisor" of the jail.

A heavy silence descended upon everyone in the room. It seemed as if they had all stopped breathing. For a long time they all stood there with their heads bent, mute and frozen.

After a long pause a voice was heard, "Go ahead and pray as much as you want."

It was the new "supervisor." A moment later he added with a sly smile, "But, at least explain to me what is it that they are saying with such enthusiasm, damn it!"

"By all means!" the young man responded. "The old man will continue, and I will explain his words in Polish, so that everyone in the room may understand."

The Seder celebration was resumed with renewed vigor. The Rosh Yeshiva began his recitation, starting from the place where he had stopped and all the Jews followed his chant:

"And it is this that has stood our fathers and us in good stead, that while not only one foe has arisen to destroy us, but in every generation an enemy rises to destroy us, the Holy One blessed be He rescues us from him!

The young man translated into Polish:

"And this, this great Faith, is what has kept the Jews going during the most difficult times of oppression, 'that not only one foe,' not only one Hitler has arisen to destroy us, but in every generation new enemies rise to wipe us off the face of the earth—"

"We, the Polish people, we too are persecuted! We also have enemies on all sides!" the chief screamer interrupted him, all excited and agitated. "Chloptzi!"* he turned to his Polish brethren who stood around him, "listen to these wise words! The main thing is not to lose faith and hope! Let's learn from them, from the *Zhidki* . . ."

"Yes, yes," the others grunted in approval. "We suffer too. We too are persecuted. . . . Why doesn't the elder of the Jews invite us to the holy ceremony. . . . We all share the same fate!"

The translator told the Rosh Yeshiva what they had said. The latter answered in a grave, measured tone:

"All people were created in the image of the Almighty. Only the murderer erases the divine image from his face. By all means, we are brothers in trouble! Squeeze together, my fellow Jews, and let's make room for our Seder guests!"

Jews and Poles sat huddled together. The Rosh Yeshiva continued his lively chant, retelling the miraculous deeds of the Exodus, and the translator told the Poles about Pharaoh and his slave society; how the Jewish slaves built Pharaoh the cities of Pithom and Ramses, and how he, Pharaoh, murdered the children of the Israelites. The Jews descended deeper and deeper into the abyss of slavery when Moses, the messenger of God, arose and saved them.

"Aha," the Poles interrupted him in excitement, "how similar that history is to what is happening around us!"

"Blood, and fire, and billows of smoke," the Rosh Yeshiva called out in ecstasy.

"And of the entire reign of Pharaoh," the translator explained, "all that was left was blood, and fire and billows of smoke . . ."

"Tak nam dapomuz bug, day Boje, day Boje," the Poles responded in great excitement, "So may the Almighty help."

"Forgive me, old man," said the loudmouthed supervisor. "You are a holy man," and he threw himself at the feet of the Rosh Yeshiva.

The old man looked at him with eyes full of compassion, and out of his thick beard came an old Hasidic folk song in Polish, a song of devotion, mixed with Hebrew words:

> On Sunday we had a feast,
> We drank plenty of wine.

---

*Boys

You must know
How to make merry,
You must know
When to quit.
Mi hulayyem
Mi shpivayem.
We make merry
We rejoice.

Slowly, all of them, the Jews and the Poles, learned the old man's Hasidic tune, and the melody passed from mouth to mouth, from heart to heart, and the entire ward resounded with brotherly, devout, soulful joy.

"Ba-a-a-m," a shot was fired, and all eyes turned to the wide open door. There stood a guard, gun in hand, mad with anger:

"*Donnerwetter,* you are having a party, eh? To bed, or I'll empty all my bullets into your heads!"

No one was afraid of him. And no one, Jew or Pole, slept all night.

It was *Layl Shimurim,* the night of Pesach, a Night of Watching. . . .

11

THE SOUND OF THE SHOFAR IN THE JUDEN LAGER

ONLY a handful of old timers among the prisoners knew about the cache inside the Nazi labor camp, and about the treasure which was kept inside of it.

The sign above the gate read *Julag*, short for *Juden Lager*, a labor camp for Jews. Such camps were not official extermination camps. There were no gallows, no gas chambers, no crematoria. To judge from the installations, the various buildings and barracks were shops equipped with sophisticated machinery. But the supervision of those camps was entrusted to the Nazi Storm Troopers, the S.S., which came to mean only one thing, and before long the camp became a mass graveyard. Even the strongest Jew could not last there for more than a few months. Small food rations, slave labor —twelve to fourteen hours a day without stop—as well as indescribable tortures—these conditions ultimately equalled the efficiency of the execution methods in even the most efficient concentration camps. The turnover of the prisoners in the camp was continuous. The dead were thrown into a huge pit, and new transports came to take their place. The predetermined fate of the newly arrived was sealed, and the camp authorities were constantly planning ahead for the new arrivals.

Only a few members of the original group of prisoners who had built the barracks and installations remained, like solitary sheaves after the harvest. The all-seeing Angel of Death must have overlooked them. Those old timers guarded a deep secret: Somewhere hidden inside the camp was a small box which contained an invaluable treasure, a rare, tiny Torah scroll, made of the thinnest parchment and written in tiny letters. Because it was so small it was easily hidden. An aged rabbi of aristocratic descent, a scion of an ancient rabbinic family, had smuggled it into the camp. Family tradition had it that the scroll came out of Spain with the Jews who were exiled by the Inquisition. The old rabbi did not live long after his arrival, but he did manage to pass his treasure on into safe hands, and it was preserved intact.

In time another sacred object was put into the box. A sexton of a synagogue arrived in one of the transports, and brought with him a shofar. Miraculously, this sexton, though weak and emaciated, survived the rigors of the labor camp. He was sure that he owed his survival to the shofar. Because of it he strove to maintain his position and continue his work as a religious functionary inside the camp. He kept track of the Sabbaths and the holidays. He held secret prayer services. He even took care of the burial of the dead.

"Jews," he whispered to his neighbors in the barracks, "the New Year is approaching. For the sake of the New Year we must form a *minyan* and pray according to our tradition."

"What's the point of a Rosh Hashana prayer without the blowing of the shofar!" one man said with a sigh.

"What's the use of blowing the shofar? What we need is the shofar of the Messiah. Oy, oy, oy, blow the great shofar for our liberation, the great sho-far, oy, oy, for our liberation—"

"We do have a shofar, we have a shofar right here!" The sexton revealed his secret in an excited whisper. "I'll bring it out and if any of you knows how to blow it, I . . ."

"Heaven forbid! No, you can't do it!" a voice of protest was heard. "I know the rules of prayer, and I am telling you that the Law prohibits us from provoking the murderers. The blowing of the shofar is an important commandment, but it does not supersede the Sabbath, and if Rosh Hashana occurs on the Sabbath you don't blow. . . . Well, this is conclusive proof. Praying can be done silently, in a still small voice, but to blow loudly is to risk our lives. Let's not endanger the people's lives by blowing the shofar!"

"But that's just the point," the sexton said with sudden intensity, "precisely because we are lost, because our lives are at the mercy of anyone who will claim them, we must blow the shofar. Our bodies are theirs, but our souls . . . we won't abandon our souls, we won't give in to them. The soul is not theirs! Jews, do you agree?"

"Yes, yes," came the answer. "If we have a shofar it's a good sign. We won't show disrespect to the shofar, heaven forbid. We will blow the shofar no matter what."

The day arrived. The dawn of Rosh Hashana. The first shift of the forced laborers left the barracks and went to work and the second shift came back from an exhausting night of work, ready for sleep. At that time the services for the Days of Awe were taking place in the hut. For this secret service the sexton prepared the shofar, having taken it carefully out of hiding. But the reading of the Torah was dispensed with. They were afraid the scroll might fall into the hands of the enemy and they decided to leave it in the cache. An expert shofar blower was found on the spot. Though he knew he was taking a greater risk than all the rest, he did not hesitate for one moment, but held the shofar firmly in his hand.

When the silent prayer began, they posted guards outside the huts. At that moment the Nazi camp guards were inside their kitchen, busily stuffing themselves with food. The sexton gave the signal, and every one in the hut held his breath.

"*Tekiah!*"

"Too-oo-oo-oo," the sound of the shofar pierced the silence and entered every heart.

"*Shevarim — teruah!*" the sexton called out in a stronger, more daring voice.

"Too-oo too-oo too-oo, tu tu tu tu tu tu tu tu," the shofar grew louder and the sound broke out and was heard throughout the camp.

"*Tekiah, shevarim, teruah!*" the voice of the sexton was heard, loud and strong, as if the sound of the shofar were breaking the arm of the wicked, subduing the villains and freeing the prisoners. . . .

"Too too too, too too too, too-too," the shofar blasted, making a deafening sound which reached the murderers who were busy stuffing themselves.

"*Kreuzdonnerwetter!* What is this? What kind of a strange alarm is this? A riot? An uprising? A signalling to the enemy? *Donnerwetter!*" The murderers jumped up and ran madly, their weapons in hand, toward the hut where the service was held.

"*Halt!* Stop!" the camp commander stormed furiously into the hut. "I caught you this time, you dirty Jews. I caught you red-handed. You are signalling our enemy with secret instruments. This is why we have had so many air raids lately, you . . ."

"Listen, listen!" a quiet and confident voice interrupted him, emanating from the crowd of worshipers.

"Shut up!" the commander shouted.

"This is no secret instrument, this is a shofar! we are praying here," one man tried to explain.

"You can't fool me, you treacherous Jews!" he screamed savagely. "We have suffered serious defeats lately. The situation on the front is very grave. The enemy's bombs hit our most vital points with deadly accuracy. It's all your fault!"

"Did you hear this, Jews? It's true!" the sexton called out, lifting up the shofar which he had taken from the blower. "True! With this shofar we signal and we bring upon you all the curses and the maledictions. I'll tell you everything, everything . . ."

"Tell, dirty Jew, tell!" the head of the murderers blurted out.

"I'll tell, I'll tell," the sexton continued in a slow controlled voice. "With this shofar we don't signal to people but to our Heavenly Father; we alert the jealous and vengeful God! The defeats you have suffered are only the beginning. We are signalling more, more . . ."

"Shut your mouth, Jew!" and in his rage the Nazi pointed his pistol at the speaker. "No, I won't shoot you. It would be a waste, a German bullet. . . . A waste! I won't finish all of you off right here on the spot. We have too few Jews left to finish off. It's a waste of good entertainment . . . you will all get your shares of whipping . . ."

Immediately henchmen attacked the emaciated Jew, and the commander himself led the execution of his orders.

As the Jew twisted and writhed in his terrible suffering, he chanted verses from the prayers of Rosh Hashana in a voice imbued with pain and exaltation.

"The righteous will see and rejoice and the upright will be glad and the pious will sing for joy—and all wickedness will vanish like smoke, for you will have removed the evil kingdom from the earth—"

The rest of the Jews, who were forced to watch his suffering, joined his prayer silently.

"And all wickedness will vanish like smoke, for you will have removed the evil kingdom from the earth—"

12

FIVE YOM KIPPUR STORIES

THE Day of Atonement, the holiest of days, underscores the essence of the Jewish people. It marks the Jews as a unique people, joining them together as one unified body. For this reason the wrath of Israel's enemies was always inflamed on that holy day. In our own time, when the archenemy of our people reared his demonic head and vowed to destroy everything that was sacred to us, he vented all his fury on the day holiest to the Jews. On that day the enemy's harshest and most fiendish designs were carried out. At the same time, he laid great schemes to force the Jews to violate the sanctity of their most hallowed day. But the Jews observed this sanctity under all circumstances, under extreme degradation and servitude, risking their lives as they secretly fasted and conducted clandestine prayer services.

In a D.P. camp in the first year of liberation a few remnants of European Jewry got together shortly before the Day of Atonement, and each reminisced on his Days of Atonement during the years of horror.

✿   ✿   ✿

The oldest Partisan spoke first:

"It was during the last manhunt which was conducted against the Jewish fugitives who were still hiding out. In my region, in Eastern Galicia, the few Jews who had not been deported to the death camps were getting caught. The number of survivors had become extremely small and the murderers' lust for blood kept growing. They searched everywhere for hidden Jews. They kept chasing the prey which dwindled day by day. The death trap was spread out everywhere. High ransoms were offered for every Jew caught alive, and many of the local peasants joined in the hunt. If there was still a chance to hide from the Germans, it had become almost impossible to escape the insidious look of the peasants who knew everyone in their neighborhood and who did not leave a single stone unturned.

"When I realized that I was the only Jew left in the entire region, I decided to walk right into the lion's den. It occurred to me, that the safest place to hide was at the home of the village priest, who was the head of all the hoodlums and murderers. I disguised myself as an old peasant, a wayfarer who walked with a limp, and I hired myself out as a day laborer at the priest's house. What helped me in lending credence to my new role was my full grown beard, streaked with grey. From time to time the Nazi pursuers searched the entire neighborhood, but it never occurred to them to search the house of their accomplice, the priest. And even the people who worked for the priest never suspected me. One time the priest's elderly maid said with a sigh, 'Ah, my old man, you are a little different from all the rest of those poor peasants, you never swear the way they do. You never curse the way they do. It's strange . . .' After that I began to force myself to swear and curse like all the rest of them.

"One time the regional head of the Gestapo came to the priest's house. I was cleaning the priest's room when that murderer walked in. I knew his face from the ghetto, and I began to shake. I shook for only a moment. I knew that any suspicious move might reveal my true identity, and I stood like a dummy with the broom in my hand. 'Father,' the Nazi said to the priest as he came in, 'I came to enlist your help in an urgent matter. Tomorrow is the Day of Atonement for Jews. I must find myself a living Jew in honor of the occasion. Last year and the year before I had Jewish men, women, children, and even rabbis at my disposal, but this year, not even one living Jew . . ." I listened to his words and I noticed that his eyes turned toward me, either intentionally or by chance. At that moment I started laughing, loudly and stupidly—and that laughter removed all suspicion from me.

"When I found out that the next day was Yom Kippur I made a vow to fast, come what may. I took my food ration to the stable where I had my bed, I gave my food to the horses, and I hummed the Kol Nidre chant to myself. There was a great deal of work at the field in the morning. They gathered potatoes, and I was sent out to help. Several workers sat around me and chewed their bread. Since I could not afford to arouse the smallest suspicion I did what the angels did at the house of our patriarch Abraham: I pretended to swallow the bread, while in effect I slipped the slices into my sleeve.

"Lunch made things even more difficult. Each worker was served a bowl of stew, and the last thing I would dare do was refuse to be served. I suddenly had an idea: I walked away to the other end of the field, and when the food distributor called my name I pretended I did not hear him—I was too absorbed in my work. Suddenly the workers began to call out from all sides, 'Hey, old man, you have missed your lunch. Your food is cold!' I came back and looked into the pot and I let out a bitter cry: 'Damn you! You expect me to eat this garbage? Hell, I won't eat it! I am going to tell the Father on you! You shameless people, taking a poor old man's food away from him!'

"I didn't touch the stew. I returned to my work with great gusto, cursing, swearing, blaspheming and working till sundown. As soon as I finished my work I hurried back to the priest and presented my complaint. I finally let myself be calmed down and agreed to received a double portion for supper. This is how I successfully completed my Yom Kippur fast under the protection of the priest. . ."

❀   ❀   ❀

The youngest of the Partisans got up and said:

"I was one of the last Jewish fighters left in the Warsaw Ghetto. Twice I had the privilege of engaging the Nazis in open battle. First in the Jewish uprising, on Passover 1943. The survivors of the

Ghetto took up arms, and the battle lasted to the last bullet. I had the good fortune to escape at the last moment through the underground sewage system to the Arian side of the city. When the general uprising of Christian Warsaw broke out in 1944, I went to war again against the Nazis. Our Jewish fighters did not pay their Polish colleagues back. We joined them in their battle. We knew that the war against the Nazi enemy was our war as well. At the beginning of the uprising a unit of Jewish Volunteers was formed. It was named after the Jewish officer who fought for Poland's freedom, Beretz Yossilewitz.

"At first the Poles were impressed by the courage of the Jewish survivors, and you could hear them voicing the historical slogan dating back to the common war of the Poles and the Jews against the Russian Czar: 'For our freedom and for your freedom.' But the honeymoon was soon over. When the Polish rebels began to suffer reverses in their uprising, they shifted the blame for their defeats to the Jewish fighters. And when the rift between the leaders of the Polish uprising and the Red Army's High Command was made known during the latter's assault on the German fort 'Warsaw,' the Jews were made the culprits. At that time many incidents occurred in which Polish rebels wantonly murdered their Jewish comrades. The Jewish fighters were consequently forced to remove their armbands bearing the letters Z.O.B. (Jewish Fighting Organization) to conceal their Jewish identity.

"In the midst of that blood bath, as we were caught up in the crossfire of the Nazi enemy outside and the Polish traitors within, one of us remembered that Yom Kippur was drawing near. We knew we were going to be the only *minyan* left in the city to pray on that Day of Atonement. . . . We were determined to hold a public prayer. And we did! In an attic of one of the military hospitals, in an aristocratic section of the Polish capital, a *minyan* of Jews gathered secretly at the risk of their lives to pray *Kol Nidre*.

"The boys came one by one, giving a password which they had gotten from a liaison person who now greeted them in uniform and in full gear. One boy came dressed as a medic, another came in bandages. We were all happy to be together that night, assembled for a prayer which united all Jews throughout the world.

"We soon became aware of one serious difficulty: We did not

have a single *machzor* or siddur, and none of the boys knew the order of the Yom Kippur eve prayers by heart. After all our searching for a prayer book failed, the order was issued for each person to write down whatever passages of the Yom Kippur prayers he happened to remember on a slip of paper.

"When the boys lined up for the *minyan,* each held in his hand a slip of paper scribbled with broken fragments of Yom Kippur prayers and hymns. The job of the *shliach tzibur,* or prayer leader was far from easy. He gathered the paper slips and joined them together as best he could to form a prayer service out of them. Never did a more incoherent and disjointed prayer reach the Throne of Glory:

> And let us forgive the entire congregation of Israel—
> We are guilty, we betrayed, we robbed, we slandered—
> Put your fear upon all your works—
> For the sin which we have sinned—
> Hear our voice O Lord our God—

"But we did feel at that moment that our prayer was pure and whole, and that it pierced the heavens. A solitary prayer in Jewish Warsaw, a great community which had been destroyed, a prayer offered by the last of her sons as they faced the horror of annihilation."

*   *   *

A young girl who survived the death camp said with a start:
"We too, in Auschwitz, saw to it that we observed Yom Kippur properly. We had to fight a tough battle for the privilege of fasting on Yom Kippur. But that was one battle which we Jewish girls, the weakest of all, did win.

"I must add that the story of our victory ends with a bitter disappointment. And when you hear about our victory and also about our disappointment, you will realize what we had to go through in that hellish extermination camp.

"Each section in the camp was separated from the others by a maze of electrified barbed wire fences. To touch the wire meant instant death. Those fences were used more than once for the purpose of committing suicide. Anyone who was tired of living would approach the fence, touch the wire, and end it all.

70

"But in spite of the lethal fence surrounding us, a good word did reach our section, the section for girls doing forced labor. The word came from a neighboring camp which was inhabited by Hungarian Jews who were slated for quick extermination. It stated that our Hungarian brothers had arranged a public prayer in their camp for Rosh Hashana, and were not stopped by the guards from doing so. That bit of news cheered us up. We discussed it and decided to determine the date of Yom Kipur according to that information and fast on that day as we were accustomed to do in the past.

"We worked out a complete plan. A few days before Yom Kippur we started working as hard as we could, without giving respite to our frail bodies. We wanted to placate our ruthless S.S. lady supervisor. Indeed, because of that effort we received a compliment from her for the first time, something to the effect of 'those industrious Jewesses.' Then, when the accursed witch was in a good mood, one of the girls, who spoke perfect German, presented a request on behalf of all the girls, which she presented with great tact and discretion.

"'Please, may we bring forth an extraordinary request: This week we Jews will observe our most important holiday. It is a fast day. Our request is that we be permitted to work only half a day, to enable the girls to fast. The remaining work hours the girls will give in advance before the holiday.'

"'Such Jewish impudence,' the Nazi supervisor exploded. 'I am too good to you, you despicable Jewesses, so you dare come to me with such requests. From here on out you will work longer hours, and in honor of your holiday you will work overtime. And don't dare fast on that day. If any of you gets too weak on that day she will be immediately sent to the crematorium. Its an order!'

"None of us was discouraged from fasting. We had decided to do it, and so we did. Some of us had come from non-observant homes and had not paid much attention to fast. But here, in the camp, they did not hesitate for a moment and were ready to join in the fast despite the danger involved. We had decided that on the day of the fast none of us would complain or show any outward sign of weakness. We would all work hard so as not to give the witch any reason to complain.

"And so it was. On that day the witch watched us constantly.

71

She inspected every girl and made sure each of us did her full quota of work. And we, the young girls, passed the test. We were physically weak, but our spirits were strong. The thought that we were joined by all the Jews in the world in our fast gave us more strength than the measly food ration apportioned to us by our enemies.

"When the fast ended, as we tasted our piece of black bread, our satisfaction was full. But the next day our joy was marred when we learned, through a secret contact with the next section, that we had miscalculated the date and missed the Day of Judgment by one day, so that we fasted on the day following Yom Kippur. How sad we were when we learned about our mistake of having eaten on Yom Kippur! But not a single girl regretted having fasted and suffered and having withstood the test. After all, our intention was pure and our devotion was total."

❋   ❋   ❋

It was the turn of the emaciated boy who looked like a yeshiva boy to speak. He said:

"My luck brought me a double slavery, one on each side of the fence. In the beginning of the War the Nazis captured me and took me to a labor camp. The purpose of the camp was not just to put Jews to work, but also to torture them and humiliate them and to invent imaginary tasks for them to do. I escaped the torture camp and found myself on Russian soil.

"The Russians decided I was a suspicious person and banished me to the wilderness of Siberia. In the Siberian exile there were many other 'suspicious' Jews like myself. We were all made to cut down trees in the primeval forests, in a nearly perpetual snow. I won't dwell on how cold it was in those parts, or on the slave labor, or on the exiles' way of life. The important thing is that Jews, wherever they are, can never forget that they are Jews, sons of Abraham, Isaac, and Jacob. If you banish them to the end of the earth, they will soon create Jewish life with all its rules and regulations. . . .

"Small wonder, then, that the Jewish exiles in the snowy steppes of Siberia remembered all the Sabbaths and all the Jewish holidays. The Russian oppressors, themselves exiles who were elevated in rank as supervisors of the Jewish slaves, could not understand the recurring demands of the Jews to be off from work because of T.S.

—T.P. (Today is Sabbath, Today is Passover). 'We don't have any holidays, except for May Day,' the Russian supervisors would say, 'and anyone who doesn't show up for work won't get his bread ration, and will be locked up.' And they added: 'Don't get too smart, Jews. We know all the tricks of your *Pops*.' The title *Pop* (a priest in Russian) was attached to any Jew who came to them with any religious demands.

"Nevertheless, when the High Holy Days approached, the rebellious mood among the Jewish slaves grew. Again and again the question was asked, 'How can they force us to violate Rosh Hashana and Yom Kippur?'

"The observant Jews were the first ones to raise the question. They urged the rest not to go to work on the Days of Awe, and their enthusiasm infected the multitudes. The word about the rebellion finally reached the ears of the supervisors. They started threatening that anyone who did not come to work on the Jews' holiday would be charged with sabotage, and the punishment for sabotage in time of war was well known. Still, many Jews did not show up for work on the first day of Rosh Hashana. The taskmasters investigated and found a synagogue in one of the cabins, where the Jews gathered for public worship. The chief overseer immediately ordered that all those who had rebelled and had gathered illegally for prayer be arrested. The order was carried out, but on the next day, the second day of Rosh Hashana, not a single Jew showed up for work in the forest. The Jews, religious and non-observant alike, were determined to fight for their rights.

"Everything turned out all right. The person in charge was a shrewd Russian peasant. When he realized how determined the Jews were, he gave in. When the Day of Atonement approached, before the Jews had a chance to ask to have the day off, he issued on order proclaiming that day, because of special circumstances, a day off for all the workers, Jews and non-Jews alike. The Jews were delighted. They rejoiced at the opportunity to celebrate Yom Kippur freely and openly among the great multitude of Siberian exiles."

❈　　❈　　❈

A Jewish soldier, a Star of David on his sleeve, added a story of his own.

"I also took part in a *Kol Nidre* prayer, which took place during the war in open defiance of the Nazis. This prayer is engraved on my heart and I shall never forget it. I was captured by the Nazis along with a large unit of soldiers from the Land of Israel. Our Nazi captors showed a special interest in us. They were at a loss, not knowing how to treat us. We did not hide our Jewishness. On the contrary, we proclaimed it openly and proudly. They could not hide their surprise and even their confusion which our proud posture caused them. They remarked more than once that we were 'Jews of a different kind,' and therefore they had to treat us differently. We quoted International Law and made our demands like soldiers speaking to soldiers, and the Nazis gave in at last and decided to treat us as such.

"When we were put into a large prisoners' camp in Upper Silesia, where the Germans held prisoners of all the Allied armies, of all races and religions, we demanded our special religious privileges as Jews. The Nazis generally recognized the demands of the prisoners in matters of religion, because of the strictness with which international institutions treated those matters. In the prisoners' camp the Jewish soldiers learned how to cherish the Sabbath, the holidays and festivals, and the memorial days. Under the oppression of the ruthless enemy we came to know the heavenly joy of the Sabbath. We began to appreciate the beauty and the glory of the Jewish holidays. Our Sabbath and holiday celebrations were attended by hosts of prisoners.

"Many non-Jewish prisoners asked for permission to attend our celebrations. Our Nazi guards took a dim view of the whole thing, but, forced to obey the international law, they did not stop them from attending.

"When Yom Kippur drew near, we decided to make that day a massive demonstration of our Jewish sovereignty even under Nazi captivity. The camp commander was told to make the largest entertainment hall in the camp available to us for the most solemn Jewish prayer observance of the whole year. They gave us the hall, and the camp administration officially announced that a 'Kol Nidre' service will be held for the Jewish prisoners. We, the prisoners from the Land of Israel, prepared the place for the service, decorating it with traditional Jewish symbols. In the meantime we found out that some of the prisoners, common soldiers as well as ranking officers from various Allied armies, who had completely forgotten about their Jewishness in the course of the year, were suddenly awakened and were expressing their desire to observe Yom Kippur with us.

"That *Kol Nidre* service was to be a demonstration of Jewish unity. In the large hall a large crowd of soldiers in the various uniforms of the Allied armies, wearing a great variety of insignia and decorations, was gathered. You could pick out British, Canadian, American, Australian, Dutch, Polish, Check, South African, Yugoslav, and other uniforms. You could see many whose Jewish identity was hardly noticeable, but at the uplifting moment of the *Kol Nidre* the Jewish sorrow could be clearly seen in their eyes. We were particularly surprised when at the last moment before the prayer began one of the highest ranking officers in the camp appeared in the hall. It had never occurred to us that he was Jewish, and he had never given us any reason to believe that he might be. Even he, the thoroughly assimilated Jew, must have had a Jewish chord hidden somewhere in his heart, and that chord must have been struck when he heard the words 'Kol Nidre'. . .

"The service was laden with emotion. The magic strains of *Kol Nidre* joined all hearts, and when the prayers were done and the people began to scatter, many of our men remained in the hall, the kind of 'common Jews' whose hearts glowed. They sat together and chanted the traditional tunes of *Kol Nidre* night. The air was filled with various versions of the *Yaale* prayer, the versions of Voholin, Poland, Habad, Galicia.

"*Yaale* . . .
May our supplications rise at nightfall,
May our cry come forth in the morning,
May our joy rise up in the evening . . ."

13

A HANUKKA CANDLE IN AUSCHWITZ

IT is said that everything depends on luck. Even for those who were taken to the gas chambers in the death camp of Auschwitz, everything depended on luck.

There were times when the executioner was in a great hurry and had no time to prolong the torture of the condemned. At such time the road from the "death cars" to the ovens was short. But on other occasions the road was unbearably long and wearisome. When the trainloads kept coming at a steady flow and the ovens could not accommodate them, the emissaries of the devil would take their time, endlessly tormenting the wretches Jews. Those emissaries were far worse than their master. Satan had invented a method of quick and efficient mass murder, while his underlings kept murdering the same people over and over again. . . .

On that snowy night the "death train" was unloaded as usual, and its new transports were led to the main entrance of Auschwitz, where the inscription could be seen above the gate, ARBEIT MACHT FREI (Work is Freedom). The chief Capo was in no rush. He did not prod the faltering marchers. He did not use his crop on their bowed heads. Nor did he use the familiar lie, "Move on, dirty Jews, move on to the big bath house. Move on!" That night the secret order from the camp commander was to direct the new arrivals to the cabins of the "labor squads" and arrange a "game" in honor of the Jewish festival, the "Festival of the Maccabees."

The brutish face of the chief Capo took on an air of anticipation, and he spoke in mock sympathy, "No rush, Jews, no rush! It's your holiday today. A good meal is waiting for you. Your bones are too dry and brittle. Can't use them to make a decent fire. In your honor we have kindled all four furnaces today, and all their chimneys will be letting out billows of smoke and tongues of fire. It is your festival of lights, *Yom Hanukka,* as you call it!"

"Hanukka!" . . . That word, spit out at the crowd by the villain, hovered in the air over the heads of the oppressed and desolate multitude, suspended like the spark that is suddenly released with a clap of thunder. Could that spark touch that extinguished clod of humanity and stir it up?

Fortunate spark!

For the greater part of the multitude the spark went unnoticed. "What is Hanukka?" But here and there someone *was* touched by it. "Hanukka? Was such a thing possible? Satan is ruling the world; there is no miracle of salvation." The spark reached them, but it died out. Only in one spot did the spark take hold and turn into a flame. "Hanukka! Hanukka in spite of it all! A single glimmer of light from the Divine Source can ultimately vanquish all darkness and evil!"

The sacred spot where the flame was kindled was in the heart of one Rabbi Efraim, the elder of the clan, the head of the court of one of the Jewish communities.

The throng moved on toward death and extinction. And in the terrible darkness the spark lit up the will to rebel. Satan was preparing for his show, intending to degrade those led to slaughter, but in the hearts of the doomed a note of dogged defiance was struck.

When the multitude was crowded into a narrow cabin too small for anyone to sit down, the old rabbi began to speak.

"My fellow Jews, it's Hanukka today! Satan himself told us so! Granted, this is an unholy place, but we mustn't neglect to kindle the Hanukka lights. We will kindle the holy Hanukka candles right here in this cabin!"

"You couldn't be serious!" someone yelled out in an anguished voice.

"Go ahead, go ahead! Light your candles. Pure olive oil and

77

ritually acceptable wicks," another person said, laughing derisively.

"Look over there," a third person cried out. "Those fires out there, they are ours, they are for us," and he pointed at the burning ovens outside the window.

"Nevertheless, today is Hanukka, my fellow Jews!" the old rabbi spoke again, raising his voice. "Who needs oil and wicks? Every Jew is a candle, even as it is written, 'The soul of man is the light of the Lord.' In the soul of every Jew there is a cruse of oil sealed with the Divine Word and reserved for a time of need. When the time comes the cruse opens, shaken by the Holy Command, and the treasured light is kindled in every Jewish soul, and the flame, the Divine Flame, begins to rise!"

The rabbi's face glowed, and sparks flew from his eyes. In his soul the cruse of oil was preserved in all its purity, and was now burning with a holy flame. It was obvious that in his great fervor the old rabbi had much more to say. But Satan in the guise of the chief Capo tore into the cabin.

"Filthy Jews, I promised you a good meal for your festival, and I am going to keep my promise! I will give you regular hotel and restaurant service—to fatten you up. But first I will teach you a lesson in the good manners we observe in this camp. Rule one: We have prepared boiling soup for you, and we will pour it into the palms of your hands. Rule two: A twenty gram slice of bread was allotted to each one of you. Every ten men will get a whole loaf and will divide it among themselves without using a knife. Rule three: Two grams of margarine will be given each one of you to-night. You will lick it off your fingers, at my order!"

The starved and degraded crowd seized upon the promise of food like a drowning man grabbing for a straw. The chief Capo and his assistants began to distribute the dabs of margarine.

"Each ration of margarine is 700 calories, enough for doing one week of work. Each pat is a day of life," the Capo expained in a methodical German tone. He was determined to squelch the last spark of humanity in the hearts of the starved inmates, and to instigate fights among them. "Every able bodied Jew will get a double portion," he added as an afterthought.

It was the turn of the old rabbi to get his portion.

"You, grandpa, I'll give you a double portion," the Capo laughed loudly, and in his mirth he dropped bits of margarine on the floor and ordered the old man to pick them up.

"A miracle, a miracle!" the old rabbi whispered. He quickly went down on his knees, carefully picked up the crumbs of fat from the floor, and put them inside the flap of his long coat.

"Ha ha ha, you old glutton," the Capo railed at the degradation of the old rabbi. The crowd of humiliated Jews stood there, failing to understand the rabbi's intention.

"The bread and the boiling soup you will get in exactly one hour. In the meantime you can lick the fat which is melting on your fingers."

The Capo left the cabin. He went to get his friends and let them share his enjoyment of watching the Jews being degraded.

"My dear friends, this is truly a miracle!" the voice of the old rabbi was heard. "I picked up the crumbs for a holy purpose. We can now light Hanukka candles! For the sake of the Hanukka candles we should be willing to give up all our margarine. I will light my portion! A miracle from heaven!"

"A Hanukka candle! A Hanukka candle!" the words aroused shouts of joy.

"To fulfill the Commandment!" the old man responded, and as he spoke he pulled some threads out of his lapel from which to make wicks and held up the flap of his coat with the bits of fat inside.

"Where will we put the fat so we can light it up?" the old man mumbled to himself, thinking out loud.

"I have a small silver spoon which I had been hiding," someone called out from the crowd.

"I will give you the cover from my pocket watch," another person said.

"Perhaps you can use the buttons from my coat?" an elegant women said as she pulled the buttons off her coat.

"Excellent idea! A true mitzvah!" The old rabbi smiled and took a few buttons. They were made of tin, and after the cloth lining was removed from them they became adequate containers for the melted fat.

All preparations for lighting the Hanukka candles were completed.

The old rabbi's face shone:

"The whole purpose of lighting the Hanukka candles is to publicize the miracle, for in the end the forces of holiness will overcome and triumph over the forces of evil and ungodliness! So, let us light the Hanukka candles on the window sill, so that the villainous enemy will know that his end is near . . ."

The old rabbi stood before the window through which he could see the smoke of the ovens rising up to heaven, and intoned the blessing over the miracle of the oil, kindling the holy flame in everyone's heart.

"These candles are holy—"

The old rabbi sang the Hanukka hymn, and many joined him in the singing.

"Rock of ages let our song—"

"*Kreuzdonnerwetter!*" the Capo came running in shouting at the top of his lungs. The light in the window had caused a general alarm.

"These are Hanukka candles. You yourself reminded us about Hanukka," the old rabbi spoke confidently, like one who had attained his goal and had nothing to fear.

"Hell and damnation! You will pay dearly for this, all of you. And you, impudent old man, you first!" the Capo screamed, his voice bristling with a disappointment, seeing that his plan had been foiled.

That night the residents of the camp tasted of the miracle of Hanukka. In their hearts, as well as in the heart of their tormentor who had vowed to take revenge, a feeling remained, a feeling that the small flickering lights on the window sill had scored a victory over the chimneys of the giant crematoria and even over death itself.

14

THE HOLY SABBATH IN THE UNDERGROUND

SABBATH the holy, Sabbath the Queen, has accompanied the Jews everywhere since they became a people. With the spreading of her wings the Sabbath Queen could transform any oppressed and downtrodden Jew into a joyous and glorious prince. Thus, the Sabbath, the soul of Judaism, became one of the prime targets of the Nazis' satanic designs. And though the Jews were harrowed because of it, they remained loyal to the Sabbath. They would neither forget nor abandon it. They brought it with them underground, they observed it in the basements and in the bunkers. Even under the worst conditions imaginable they would not let the splendor of the Sabbath dim.

❁　　　❁　　　❁

"Remember the Sabbath, children! For heaven's sake, do not forget!"

It was Mother's pleading voice. A voice laden with sorrow, yet full of love and compassion.

It was Monday—a trying day in the life of the ghetto. On Monday the Nazi authorities handed out the weekly bread rations. It was part of the scheme. Once a week the Jew was handed out his entire weekly ration, and it was up to him to divide it into seven little portions, to eat his bread little by little, a few crumbs at a time . . . if he couldn't control himself he would eat it all in one day and would be left to die of hunger. The adults learned how to divide their bread into daily portions. But the famished children had a harder time of it.

"Oh, Mother, we can't do it. We can't divide our bread. Please, Mother dear, do it for us!" they pleaded.

And Mother, the most wretched creature in the world, bore the pain of the entire family. The unhappy task of dividing and distributing the bread to the children for the entire week became hers. It was no easy job. She would slice the loaf into as many thin pieces as she possibly could, and as she weighed and passed out the slices she made sure a few were saved up for the Sabbath.

"Remember, children, the days fly by, and before you know it the holy Sabbath comes, knocking on the door. Please remember!"

In her own heart the mother knew how hard it was to reserve a slice of bread for the end of the week. So she took it upon herself to keep the bread for her little ones.

"Listen, children, I am the one who is keeping the portion for the Sabbath. Each one of you will put aside as much bread as he wants for the Sabbath and will hand it over to me for safe keeping!"

"Very well, Mother. We'll do as you say!" several voices responded together. One of the children, who lay sick in bed, asked in a hesitant and shy voice,

"If we all give up a slice of bread for the Sabbath, would you make us a delicious pudding like you did last Sabbath?"

"God willing, God willing," Mother said in a whisper, as if praying.

"Hey, yes, Mama. How did you make that wonderful kugel?" one of the children cried, suddenly remembering the taste of that delicious Sabbath pudding.

"I won't give away my secret," Mother smiled. She recalled how she had prepared the kugel and she blushed.

Mother did not reveal her secret recipe. What was there to reveal? She had saved up some crumbs from her daily ration of bread and performed a "miracle." But now that her little son had taken sick she began to share her ration with him, and it looked doubtful at best that she might be able to come through again with a pie.

"Next Sabbath you will eat a good kugel, God willing," she said, wrapping a few slices of bread with her trembling hands in a white Sabbath cloth. "I promise you, it will be a very good kugel, children!"

And she kept her promise.

Indeed, such a Sabbath pudding was never baked before. It was a pudding fit for a king! She had gathered potato peels and hid them like a treasure. When no one was looking she immersed them in water, washed them clean, then dried them and ground them in a hand mill. To this she added salt, pepper, roasted barley, bran, and spicy herbs. Another condiment which she added to this mix were her own hot tears.

"May it be Your will," she prayed in her heart, "may it be Your will that my children enjoy this kugel as much as our ancestors enjoyed the manna in the desert. May it be Your will, Master of the world, that my pudding do honor to the Sabbath."

But while the poor woman was busy preparing the pudding, a nagging thought kept haunting her like a bothersome fly: Who knows, perhaps she was desecrating the Sabbath by making a pie out of throwaway potato peels?

"Perhaps I ought to add a few drops of oil to this strange concoction," she wondered. "Oil will give it flavor. But if I use the oil for the pudding, what will I use for kindling the Sabbath lights?"

She agonized over the question: food and candles, both in honor of the Sabbath. Which should come first?

There is no doubt that the Sabbath candles come first, for we are commanded "to kindle a Sabbath light," a commandment over which we make a blessing. . . .

But what good will a candle light do for a dying child? It is a matter of life and death. A pudding baked with some oil could revive him; it could save his life!

Her heart fluttered and skipped a beat, and her arguments continued. . . . The mitzvah of candle lighting could also save the child. The boy needs the mercy of Heaven, and God is never more receptive to a Jewish woman's prayer than when she blesses the Sabbath candles. At that moment a new thought crossed her mind. A daring thought: She will bless the Sabbath lights without any oil in the containers! He who dwells on high and knows the thoughts of man's heart will understand her intentions. . . . He will know that she dedicated her last drops of oil in honor of the Sabbath by helping to save a life, and that she would kindle the light without oil, without flame. . . .

On Sabbath eve, at twilight, the woman stood facing her empty oil lamps in which the singed wicks of last week lay, and her lips whispered an innocent prayer:

"Master of All the Worlds, accept my Sabbath lights, which are without flame, and in Your great mercy, kindle them with Your supreme light. Heavenly Father, forgive a poor woman who stole the oil from the lamps to kindle the joy of the Sabbath in the hearts of her children who are dying before her very eyes. And if I am not deserving, and if my prayer will go unanswered, attune Your ears, merciful Father, to the songs of the holy Sabbath which each child, including the sick one, will sing in my poor home when I put the Sabbath pudding on the table . . .'

The kugel was served. The children ate it, tasting paradise, and they sang,

> *Mizmor shir le'yom ha'Shabbos* . . .
> A hymn, a song for the Sabbath . . .

And Mother? Mother swallowed her choking tears, mixed with joy and fear, and she did not notice at all how the Sabbath Queen herself spread her pristine wings over the joyous children, joining them in the song,

A hymn, a song for the Jewish mother!

✿   ✿   ✿

Reb Sholem Shachna, whom the Germans dubbed Herr Spitznadel, or Mr. Needlepoint, paced rhythmically around the large room. He was the chief tailor of the ghetto, and headed the Jewish workers doing forced labor for the German occupation army. As he paced the floor of the workshop he waved his wooden ruler, conducting the workers like a cantor conducts his choir:

'On the Sabbath, on the Sabbath, on the Sabbath, on the Sabbath, on the Sabbath day . . ."

The workers in the room, old and young, sat poring over their sewing machines, keeping time to the singing,

"On the Sabbath, on the Sabbath . . ."

Suddenly Sholem Shachna the tailor stopped pacing, stood in the middle of the room, and with an odd expression of stern apprehension and frightened determination called out,

"Listen everybody! When that son of the devil appears, you spin your wheels at top speed! Otherwise you will be the living end of me, you bums!"

"Take it easy, Reb Sholem Shachna. Have some respect! After all, our rabbi sits here!" The limping sexton had jumped up, and was now pushing aside the sewing machine and waving in protest. "And who allowed you, Reb Sholem Shachna, to violate the Sabbath in public?"

"Rabbi, Rabbi, heaven forbid," the startled Reb Sholem carefully approached the old rabbi who sat behind the first sewing machine in the room. 'I only mean to spin the wheels without ever threading the needles. Just pretend and make believe, to pacify that so and so."

"Even this is strictly forbidden, strictly forbidden!" the petulant sexton blurted out again. "Let the rabbi speak and tell us what the Law says!"

"The saving of a life is involved here! The Sabbath can be overlooked when life is in danger, as the Rabbis have taught!" The old rabbi expressed his opinion, speaking calmly and emphatically.

"But I, rabbi," Sholem the tailor said apologetically, "I can't fool that so-and-so all by myself. He purposely checks on us on the Sabbath to make sure we do not observe our holy day! He purposely comes on the Sabbath to get the new uniform which I've made for him. I will iron it in front of him, but the iron will be cold, rabbi, I swear, it will be cold, I will only pretend . . ."

"You have no choice. I trust you, Reb Sholem!" the old rabbi said, peering up at the tailor with soft and approving eyes.

"He is a great man, our rabbi is," Sholem said exaltantly and took his seat at the main table. It was a moment of reconciliation and reparation for Sholem Shachna Spitznadel the tailor. The whole ghetto was envious of him, but what did he do to deserve it? He was a born tailor. A tailor son of a tailor. In his family the thread and the needle were handed down from generation to generation. In his childhood he learned how to sew dress uniforms, and his fame spread. The commander of the ghetto, the archvillain, was extremely fond of fashionable clothes, and thus Sholem Shachna won a place in his heart. In fact it was he himself who appointed the master tailor Spitznadel as the supervisor of forced sewing and tailoring.

But Sholem Shachna did not abuse his powers. On the contrary. He used it to recruit the old rabbi, the two judges, the *rosh yeshiva* and even the lame sexton as helpers for his shop, thus saving all of them from calamity and from evil decrees.

"Master of the Universe, give me strength to withstand temptation," the chief tailor mumbled to himself, as his trembling fingers smoothed the new uniform he had sewn for that wicked son of the devil.

"Haman is coming! Haman is coming!" Sholem's call of alarm rang throughout the room and made everyone tremble. "Get up everybody—before he comes in!"

A kick on the door resounded, and in stormed the archenemy.

"*Kreuzdonnerwetter, aufstehen!* (Damn it! Stand up!)" he howled. His murderous face twisted when he realized the Jews had already been standing at attention.

"Sir, we don't have time to stand idly," Sholem Shachna Spitznadel broke the silence, turning about the cold iron and smiling discreetly.

"No jokes, dirty Jew! My Jews do not joke!" the enemy continued to howl. "Answer briefly. Is everything ready?"

"Everything is ready, sir!" Sholem Shachna answered with a bow, and added meekly, "May I tell the men to go back to work? There is no time to waste!"

"You are right, you, dirty Jew! You are a clever man," he added, softening his voice.

All the sewing machines were humming again. The wheels spun without threads, pretending to work. Sholem Shachna quickly and expertly began to fit the new uniform on the obese body of the ghetto commander.

"Commander, Sir, when you are promoted I will make you an even better uniform," Sholem Shachna said as he continued to work.

"Shut up, Jew! Who told you I was about to be promoted?"

"Commander, Sir, I only guessed. To judge from the way you tortured the Jews I figured you had it coming to you!" Sholem Shachna spoke with thinly disguised irony, keeping a straight face all the while.

"Ha ha, wretched Jew! You *are* smart. You guessed right," the German guffawed.

He had finished putting on his new uniform and he could not conceal his admiration for that masterful creation.

"Come here!" he ordered the tailor. He scrutinized the Jewish tailor's strained face and yelled with incomprehensible anger,

"Say, are you really a Jew? It must be a dirty lie!"

"Sir? A Jew? Of course I am a Jew just like all the rest of the workers here. Here, ask anyone of them."

"It can't be true! A Jew couldn't do such fine work! I know that all Jews are thieves, peddlers, cheaters and exploiters!" the German yelled, and in his rage he tore the yellow star off the tailor's sleeve.

"No, you are not a Jew! You are a master craftsman, not a Jew! Look at all those helpers of yours, can they do this kind of work?" and he turned his murderous gaze at the Jews in the room who kept spinning their wheels without stop.

Sholem Shachna sensed the danger in the air and hastened to save the situation.

"Sir, may I ask you, do you smoke?"

"Shut up, impudent Jew! You don't expect me to offer you a cigarette, do you? You'd better watch out, you damned Jew!"

"You are mistaken, sir. Today is the Sabbath, and I am not allowed to smoke," Sholem Shachna smiled, and with a deft gesture he pulled a golden cigarette box out of the drawer of his worktable.

"Commander, Sir, please forgive my saying so! It occurred to me that this cigarette box will go well with this uniform."

"Damned Jew, you are clever indeed." And he quickly slipped the shiny box into his pocket. Sholem Shachna had been successful.

"I am finished for now. I have no more time to waste," the German said hastily and left the room.

"*Danke schön* (thank you kindly), Commander, Sir." Sholem Shachna accompanied the villain to the door.

"Thank God for small favors," Reb Sholem said when he came back, trying to cheer up the frightened Jews.

"On the Sabbath, on the Sabbath, on the Sabbath, on the Sabbath day!"

"On the Sabbath, on the Sabbath—" the wheels kept spinning in time to the Sabbath song.

       ✿   ✿   ✿

"What day is today? Friday? Saturday? Or is it Sunday already?" The question was asked by three people. All three had been hiding in the bunker, in the foul, musty, underground air. They were aroused from a deep sleep fraught with nightmares which had lasted since . . . since when? Each had a different recollection. They all agreed that it started before the Sabbath. Now that they woke up they could not decide how long that strange sleep had lasted. They kept arguing.

One of them said:

"I remember exactly what happened. We had lit our stove and we cooked a stew for the Sabbath. The smell of the stew put us to sleep. In my sleep the odor of the food intoxicated me. I could tell it was daytime but I couldn't wake up. Today is the Sabbath, I could swear to it!" His friend disagreed:

"Oh, no. You were dreaming. We only slept for a few hours. We lit the stove, as I recall, in the morning, the morning of Friday. We all went to sleep immediately. The day is still young. We have time to prepare for the Sabbath."

"With your permission, gentlemen," the voice of a young girl was heard. The bunker dwellers referred to her by the endearing name "Dvorale." "I believe both of you are mistaken. We passed a long, long night. I woke up a few times and I was very frightened. I called out a few times but no one answered. I fell asleep again, and now, look outside! It's very quiet outside, not a single German anywhere. It must be Sunday, when they have the day off to entertain themselves, and they leave us alone."

This conversation took place in one of the last bunkers of the demolished Warsaw Ghetto. The participants were the "Jews of the Ruins," those few who had insisted on staying alive. Some continued to live under the ruins of the Ghetto, after everything had been reduced to ashes and soot. There were two kinds of "Jews of the Ruins"—those who found refuge in deep bunkers underground, and those who hid in the "upper" bunkers, in various hiding places in the skeletons of the half-burned buildings. The latter kind of hide-outs had many shortcomings, as they had none of the provisions that could be found in the underground bunkers. But they had the advantage of providing observation positions which enabled their residents to look out for search squads of the murderers who kept looking untiringly for the remnants of the Jews.

"We must have 'swallowed' the Sabbath in this nightmarish sleep of ours," the two grown-ups conceded to the logic of the young girl. For indeed there was no sign outside of any Nazi search teams. On the other hand, the neighborhood crawled with packs of Polish 'Hyenas,' scavengers who poked in the ruins in search of valuables which could be removed from the dead bodies of those Jews who were buried under the debris. The great day for those scavengers was Sunday, when no one stopped them from searching the ruins.

"So what if we slept a day or two? I wish we could sleep forever," one of them said with a sigh of despair.

"It's my fault!" the other rejoined. "I found a bottle with some strange liquid in it and I thought I could use it to light the stove. It must have been poisonous. It's a miracle we are still living."

"It's too bad about the Sabbath we have lost, especially since I had prepared a big surprise for you!" said Dvorale, the little housewife of the bunker.

"Tell us what it is, Dvorale," the two of them, Menachem, her older brother, and Label, his friend, urged her.

"I'll tell you, but on the condition you will be willing to wait till next Sabbath."

And she told them she had discovered some rice scattered on the floor of the basement of one of the burned out buildings. She cleaned it up, removing splinters of glass, and was going to make a stew out of it. Now, she concluded, she would make it for the following Sabbath and give each one an additional portion for the lost Sabbath.

In the darkness of their ebbing life, those hounded and famished people who lived like rats saw a new light rekindled, the light of the holy Sabbath. Like rats, they had to hide from the light of day. In the daytime they lay still on their beds, careful not to make the slightest move because of the enemy prowling outside, listening to detect any suspicious sound with his special electronic devices. At nightfall, when the manhunters left in fear of being assaulted by the remnants of the Jewish rebels, the muffled activity began throughout the ghetto hide-outs. Like starved animals the Jews would crawl out of their holes. Since the uprising a few secret food depots remained under the ruins. Those depots were the targets of the surviving Jews. They were frequently successful in finding them. Inside those stores they found musty bread, wormy grits, stinking, rotten potatoes. All of this meant life, and each choice find was saved up for the Sabbath. The anticipation of the Sabbath was enough to keep everyone going during the rest of the week.

"You, Dvorale, prepare the stew, and I'll be sure to get wine for Kiddush," said Menachem, Dvorale's older brother.

"Who will get us firewood? You can't make a stew without coals," Dvorale said calmly.

"I'll take care of it," gloomy Label said.

They each kept their promise.

At midnight Label brought a smoldering beam into the hide-away. He boasted,

"Here is coal 'plus'! The burnt part we can use for coals. The unburnt part we can cut up into small pieces to suck on when we begin to suffer from thirst."

"Don't look at the pot but what's inside it!" Menahem said one day as he came in holding a moldy pot full of water. "The water is pure!"

It was a great find, a priceless treasure! During the Warsaw Ghetto uprising, the German murderers cut off all water to the Ghetto. Water lines were blown up, wells were destroyed, and water supplies were poisoned. The remnants of the Jews in the Ghetto would drink rain water which was stored in the mud. But this source had dwindled during the heat wave, and now, surprise! A pot of water!

"I promised to get wine for Kiddush," Menahem boasted. "I risked my life and got a pot full of water."

The Sabbath meal in one of the last bunkers of the decimated Ghetto was complete: Kiddush over a glass of moldy water, and a rice stew instead of meat and fish and the other customary Sabbath delicacies. . . .

The Sabbath meal made them drowsy. This time they enjoyed their sleep. The last survivors of the Holocaust slept peacefully, protected by the Holy Sabbath's Angels of Peace.

15

THE CURSE OF THE OLD PARTISAN

T HE remnants of the devastation sat together, with no place to go. Each bore the weight of his individual suffering. Each longed to pour out his tale of woe. It was as if the burden each suffered was too great for him alone, but by sharing it, by weaving a single fabric of the various memories, together they would lift the shroud of sorrow that enveloped them.

The first to speak was the old Partisan. He was excited and vociferous, and they all listened to him out of respect for his age.

"They say that memory is our enemy, our downfall. Let's face it, we are all afraid to confront the horrible shameful memories of our past. . . . But I tell you, I am not afraid! Not on your life! And I'm not ashamed! Me, I am a spiteful man. I swear to you, we have nothing to be ashamed of. Let each of us dig deep into those horrible memories and chances are he will come up with something pure and precious, something in which there can be no shame. . . .

"Like I said, I am a spiteful man! I have always been accustomed to do things out of spite. Because of this I have survived. Everything I ever did would strike people as odd and bizarre. All the Jews ran away from the ghetto to look for a place to hide. They fled to the forests, they hid in caves. But, I for spite went out and mixed among the gentiles, and I was lost amidst their hustle and bustle. Other Jews had shaved their beards and their earlocks. Me, I did just the opposite. I kept my beard. Not one hair did I shave.

I owe my life to my beard. It stood me in good stead, except that it turned white. I had entered the ghetto a young man and I came out a grey-beard. No one is a greater expert at dying hair than the Angel of Death. He took one look at me and I turned grey. Once I became an old man he left me alone. What's the hurry? I was his now. He knew I could never get away from him. . . .

"But as I said before, I am a spiteful man. I was startled to see my face framed by a white beard, but I kept it all the same. Another Jew in my place would have run away to hide in a pit or a cove or a rat hole. Me, I carried my beard with dignity. I would squat at the door of the church, I would genuflect and cross myself incessantly like a pious and devout gentile, stretching out my hand and asking for charity. The Ukrainian peasants, murderers sons of murderers, descendants of the archmurderer Hmelnitzky, may he roast in hell, they, the peasants, believed that all I wanted was some charity—but what I was really begging them for was life—for a day or even a moment of life. Every breath I took in those days was as a gift. . . . This is why I posed as a beggar outside their church, after my right to live as a Jew had been taken away from me.

"I used to tease the Angel of Death. Not only did I refuse to hide from him, I would actually look him straight in the eye. The Ruthinian priest in the village was the chief murderer of the Jews, and I, an old beggar limping, knocking on doors, constantly reciting prayers—I looked for shelter and sustenance at the house of that honorable priest. . . . While all around me the place crawled with ruffians and cut-throats, I found myself a haven at the home of that rabidly anti-semitic priest, and from there I tried to establish contact with the Partisans.

"When the extermination campaign was over, and the last of the Jews in our region was dead, the murderers became angry. They were lusting for more Jewish blood, but there was none left. All the Jews were gone. I was caught in the clutches of the devil, but I was not afraid. Satan and his minions were clever, but who was going to suspect an old, crippled, pious beggar who served the priest with such great devotion?

"Once I almost got caught. It was because of that Jewish feeling of solidarity, a feeling which never dies. I had always dreaded meeting Jews. I felt that if I ever did meet any, the last ones left,

92

I might break down and my entire façade would crumble. And sure enough, I did meet some fellow Jews! That day I was busy working in the priest's fields with a group of peasants, gathering an abundant harvest of vegetables. When the wagon was full we prepared to return to the village. A young wagon driver, himself a peasant, held the reigns while I sat in the rear looking backward. I guarded the vegetables, which were worth their weight in gold. Suddenly, without any forewarning—a band of Jewish forced laborers appeared on the road coming in our direction. Living Jews? Not exactly. They were walking shadows, moving haltingly. They were the last remnant of a large slave camp, who could well have been heading for their last destination. My heart skipped. I almost jumped off the wagon and ran to join them. Could I keep myself apart from them? Why shouldn't I share their destiny? And why wait until I found my own lonely fate? But, since I was a spiteful man by nature, I decided at the last minute to remain spiteful. No, I did not jump off the wagon. I didn't budge. My heart pounded, and I knew I had to do SOMETHING, I had to react, relieve my emotions, vindicate myself. . . .

"An idea came into my head. I began to curse those Jews. As I cursed them I was thinking of a way to distribute the priest's vegetables among them. I kept shouting curses at those wretches like a good Ukrainian peasant, and I accompanied my shower of curses with a shower of vegetables which I started to pelt them with, using both hands. I shelled them with beets, carrots and other vegetables. I kept throwing and cursing. And the Jews? At first they recoiled, trying to dodge the missiles. They must have thought that I was throwing stones at them. When they looked back they realized it was vegetables. They slowed down, and began a harvest of their own. When I saw this, I kept throwing more, until I half-emptied the wagon.

"To tell the truth," the old Partisan concluded his story with a deep sigh, "to this day, whenever I think of it, I cry inside. I don't know what my poor brothers thought of me at that moment. They must have taken me for a wicked and heartless person, who thought nothing of wasting priceless food to badger and torment a band of lost Jews. They must have thought that, and their last curse must have been saved up for me. It must have been . . ."

16

TWO JEWESSES AND ONE BOTTLE OF BRANDY

THE old Partisan grew silent as he wiped away a tear. A blonde girl, who was called "Shikse" by everybody because of her perfectly Arian looks, seized on the opportunity and began to talk.

"As long as we are reminiscing, let me tell you how a fellow Jewess was able to fool me. I was sure she was a high born Polish Arian, but I found out she was a Jewess just like myself. She was an extremely clever woman. She took one look at me and she knew who I was. But how could she know? I was born blonde. I never had to dye my hair, and the gentile girls were envious of me. I felt secure that no one could suspect me. Yet she, she . . . on the first day we met—

"She was the supervisor of the factory where I started to work. She looked right into my eyes, and I almost died. She didn't say anything at the time. She didn't ask me for any documents. She never mentioned the word *Jiduvka* (Jewess). Softly and quietly she asked me, 'Why are you so sad?' In those days such a question meant certain death. In those days anyone who looked worried or sad was suspected of being a Jew. Gentiles were enjoying themselves as never before. A world of lawlessness had opened up before them, and they were having the time of their lives. Robbery

94

and murder in broad daylight had become the order of the day, and the more depraved a person was, the more successful he was. No shame, no fear of punishment. Anyone who was afraid to rob and kill was considered a coward. . . . The Arian supervisor was right. I had no business being sad. A blonde, gentile girl, sad?

"My sorrow was going to be the end of me. I relied too much on the color of my hair to get me through. The Polish I spoke was perfect. Perhaps too perfect, which might have aroused suspicions. Only Jewish girls strove to speak perfect Polish. I tried to corrupt my speech, to make mistakes, to mix in common curses. It was very hard for me to swear, but I did it. Everything was in perfect order. My papers were perfectly legal. They were the papers of a gentile woman who was killed when the war broke out. But my heart remained a Jewish heart, and kept drawing me to places where my people were in danger. I found no rest. Because I lived like a gentile, and pretended to be one of them, my heart ached all the more for my brothers. My feet kept carrying me to the walls of the burning ghetto. I could not stay away. Was there any wonder I was so sad? Sorrow became my constant companion, and perhaps would remain so forever. . . .

"Who can count the casualties of the burning ghetto? Even on the other side of the walls, outside the ghetto, the victims were numerous. The blood thirsty peasants received a bounty for every Jew they captured and brought in alive. Their job was quite easy. The ghetto was going up in flames and the flames, like a magnet, drew many Jews hidden among the gentiles to the ghetto. I was drawn too, like all the others, hoping that I could do something to help rescue some of the victims who were trapped by the fire. The Nazis and their protégés lay in wait around the ghetto, behind the walls, and they found me there. 'Lady, why are you so sad to see the ghetto go up in flames?' A Nazi secret agent interrogated me. 'Aren't you happy to see those Jew bastards roasting?' I almost got caught this time. But luck smiled upon me again—I came up with a quick explanation for my sorrow. 'How can I be happy when part of my property was left in the ghetto? I was foolish enough to entrust it to some smugglers. . . . If you had waited a few days with the burning of those damned Jews I would have been able to retrieve my property. . . .' A goodly sum of money which I happened to have at that moment helped convince the Nazi that I was telling the truth. I put it in his hand as the two of us shared our contempt for those wretched brothers and sisters of mine in the crumbling, smoldering ghetto.

"Coming back to my factory supervisor when she became aware of all that pain and sorrow in my Jewish heart, I was sure the mask had come off my face and I was doomed. I was ready to walk over to her and yell in her face, 'I am a Jewess!' and get it over and done with once and for all. But the woman was kind and understanding. She was a compassionate and noble soul. She told me not to be sad. She was looking for ways to cheer me up. She would tell me jokes and try to make me laugh. Once she invited me to her room and closed the door after me. It was after work hours, and I had happened to stay late. I entered her office. To my surprise she locked the door, and proceeded to take out a large bottle of brandy and put it on the table. 'Don't be sad. Drink!' she ordered me. Before I could grasp what was happening she opened the bottle and took a long drink. Again she told me to drink, and added, 'I, too, at times have to chase my sadness away. These are personal, private matters.' She laughed, and then she forced me to take a drink. I started to take brandy regularly from that time on. At times I would actually become drunk. It worked. I became happy and gay like all the rest of the gentiles around me. No one suspected me any longer. The supervisor did not bother me any more. She took no interest in me, but when the Nazi inspectors came into the factory she always pointed me out as an example of loyalty and dedication . . .

"I am ashamed to admit it . . . she had fooled me. She, too, was Jewish. After the war, when every surviving Jew began to look for his former helpers and benefactors, I found out that this woman who helped save me was herself Jewish, and she, a Jewess, had forced me to drink and get drunk. I had bumped into her in the street by accident. I recognized her, and she abandoned her masquerade. Our meeting took place in a deserted street in the ruins of liberated Warsaw. 'Mrs. Malgojata!' I held her hand and tried to kiss her. I was very excited when I recognized her. 'Mrs. Malgojata, thanks to you I am alive! You are the only noble Polish woman I ever met.' She laughed at my words. 'Silly girl,' she said. "What makes you think I am a shikse? I refused to believe her. She shouted out *Shema Yisrael*. I still refused to believe her. She retorted, 'You foolish girl, you were saved by a Jewess, who had saved other Jews like yourself by getting them all drunk and keeping them happy.' I began to understand the whole plot. She worked at the factory and served the Germans in order to save Jews. The worst informer was Jewish sorrow—any Jew could be spotted by his sad eyes—and 'Mrs. Malgojata' chased away that destructive sadness by forcing every Jewish worker in the factory to drink and forget the terrible catastrophe. . . .

"I was so angry with her," the blonde girl said as she finished her story, "for not giving me any hint of her Jewishness, but I was happy to know that the noble woman who had saved my life was Jewish after all . . ."

17

BROTHERLY HELP THAT ENDED
IN A COMMON GRAVE

MEMORIES are like a fabric. Each thread is interwoven with other threads, and when one is pulled out, others come loose. . . . The thread of the story was seized upon by the youngest member of that group of survivors. He was still a child, hardly an adolescent, but his manner of speech belied his childish appearance.

"I am the youngest one here, but what I have seen, I am sure none of you ever saw. You, grownups, you stayed put most of the time, so what could you have seen? We children, we couldn't sit still in the ghetto. We sneaked out, over the wall, to look for food; we got in touch with the Poles and got them involved in the smuggling business. We slipped out of the ghetto under the very noses of the Gestapo guards, laughing in their filthy faces. We were young, but weren't children. We knew and understood everything perfectly well. When we began to suffer from hunger in the ghetto I couldn't sit still and do nothing. Father and Mother were very hungry. Grandmother was hungry too. I got up in the middle of the night and went out to find food. My parents did not say anything. They were too weak, too starved. . . . Only grandmother spoke out. She begged me not to go. She swore that even if I did come back and bring food she wouldn't so much as taste it. She kept her word. I went out and returned the next day. On the way I crossed several barbed wire fences. No matter. Barbed wire stands only in the way of cowards. I brought back food, a sack full of potatoes. My parents were very pleased. But not grandmother. She wouldn't taste it. She cooked for my parents who were sick, but she wouldn't put anything in her own mouth. 'Blood,' she said. 'These potatoes are dripping blood.' No matter what I said to her she wouldn't listen. 'No,' she kept saying, 'you'd better stay home and not risk your life. Whatever becomes of all the Jews will become of us.'

"Grandmother cried and said that I was only a child. But I wasn't a child at all. I was really a little man. I knew everything. I knew all the farmers, which one sold what, and which ones I should avoid. I knew the right time to drop in on a farmer without being seen by his neighbors, and I knew what each farmer wanted me to bring him from the ghetto. This one wanted a wrist watch. This one wanted a pair of boots. This one wanted gold coins, those Russian gold coins which the Jews dubbed 'Pigs.' This one wanted paper money in denominations of 500 zlotes, and this one only wanted old bills from before the War. I took some children along as helpers. They, too, were not really children. We arranged everything. We got flour, sugar, beans, vegetables. Sometimes we even got milk for the little children in the ghetto. I once brought milk and even grandmother drank it. She was very sick at the time. Father had died. Mother had pulled herself together and recovered. My earnings I gave to Mother to hide, but some money I kept, and hid outside the ghetto, in some ruins. But I didn't tell Mother. I couldn't tell anyone. Only my friends knew. They also hid things. They knew my hiding place and I knew theirs. We had a sort of a brotherhood, born out of trouble. . . .

"And then one day, all business suddenly stopped. The farmers had gotten together and decided not to sell us anything. They did not hide the bitter truth from us. They simply told us that it didn't pay for them to sell to us any more. After all, the Germans had promised them the entire ghetto. The Germans said that all the Jews were going to be deported and killed, and the ghetto would remain the property of the Polish people,—the houses, the furniture, everything. Even the things that were hidden underground.

"I went to look for food elsewhere. Our ghetto was on the border between Galicia and Hungary. I went there to buy or 'borrow' something. In the warehouses on the border there was plenty of food. Our farmers used to steal a great deal from those warehouses. Once when I was walking among the Hungarian soldiers on the border I suddenly saw some Jews. Jews on the other side of the border. They were not soldiers. They had no weapons. They were forcer laborers dressed in a special uniform. They spoke of *Munka Tabor,* which in Hungarian meant labor camp. Those Jews mixed Hungarian words in their Yiddish, like *teshek,* which meant 'please.' They realized I was a Jewish boy and they were afraid to approach me. The Gestapo kept a close watch on them. Only after great difficulties was I able to make contact with them. They lived inside a fenced barracks. I went there at night and told them about the ghetto, and how people were dying there of starvation every day, and how the farmers had decided not to sell us any food.

"Oh, those Jewish laborers! They, too, were in trouble. They were worked to death, they weren't given much to eat, and they were frequently beaten up. How the Hungarian officers knew how to beat them! But when those unfortunates heard how bad things were in the ghetto they wept. They were all ready to help us. They decided to leave us some of their meager daily portions. They left soup in their kitchen for the starving Jews of the ghetto. There were several hundreds of them, and they all decided to eat a little less each day. There were no guards at night, because the Hungarian soldiers who guarded them would go out on the town after dark, and whoever came over from the ghetto at night was able to help himself to some food. . . .

"Those laborers lived up to their decision. They were weak and hungry, yet they left something to eat in the kitchen every day. It was not easy to sneak out of the ghetto and go to the border. Not everyone could do it. Only a few people knew about it and tried to make the trip. They were mostly children who crawled under the barbed wire at night for a chance to fill their belly. The soup wasn't too bad. It had grits and bones, and at times even whole potatoes. There were work squads in the ghetto that went out to work in the fields every day. The workers learned how to sneak into the barracks at night. I was the main organizer of those activities. I found the way to get there, I was the liaison and I provided the necessary information.

"What happened later on I find very hard to talk about. It was awful. The Gestapo laid a trap for the *Munka Tabor* Jews and our whole scheme was discovered. One night they surrounded the kitchen in the barracks and found some of the famished Jews who had come from the ghetto for some hot soup. Those ghetto Jews were murdered where they stood along with quite a number of the forced laborers who had committed the crime of feeding their starved brothers. And now, my friends, please give me your verdict. Am I to blame for that murder? You, grownups, please tell me. True, I drew the Jews into this whole trap, but they knew what risk they were taking. They knew they were taking their lives in their hands helping the Jews of the ghetto. Am I to take the entire blame upon myself?

"Our ghetto was completely destroyed. No one remained alive. The Germans kept their promise to the farmers. I hid at the last moment and I was spared. Only one other child was saved. The starved Jews of the ghetto who were caught and murdered did not lose anything. They were doomed from the start. Perhaps they even gained something, in that they were buried in a common grave, properly dug. In the ghetto no one was given proper burial. I don't know where my mother is buried. The grave of those who were murdered at the border has remained, and its place is known. The Jews of the *Munka Tabor* were buried in the same grave. They were all buried together. Am I to blame for their death? Those Jews might have been spared. . . . The forced laborers were not exterminated, like those in the ghetto. Many of them survived. Who knows, perhaps I was the cause of their death. I started the whole thing. I got them involved in it. Tell me, was it my fault? . . ."

18

THE CONFESSION OF A BEREAVED FATHER

THE CRY of pain of the surviving child touched the heart of the most taciturn person in the group like a spark set to gunpowder. He was always tight lipped, and his teeth were always clenched. Only the deep wrinkles on his high forehead revealed that his silence was the result of a supreme effort to overcome an inner voice which might burst out at any moment.

The wall of silence was cracked, and the man began to talk in a stutter.

"If there is anyone here who is guilty, it is I! I am the murderer! I have murdered my own children! It was almost as if I murdered them with my own hands! What shall I say? Will anyone understand me? Could it be that I did the right thing? Who will decide? Who will judge me? No, I won't tell."

"I won't tell! No way!" the taciturn person repeated his words in a pitiful voice. But the rest of them knew that the spring of suffering had opened, and the man was going to tell everything, revealing the wounds in his heart.

"What shall I tell you? What have I got to say? We were like monkeys. We were hunted animals, and that's how we lived. Monkeys in the jungle build their homes on trees, but we were lower than them. We dug a pit under an old decaying tree and lived in it. For years we lived on herbs and weeds. Nuts and mushrooms were our delicacies. We learned to distinguish between all the different kinds of herbs in the forest. There were some herbs which were fat and juicy and very tasty. Others were thorny and bitter and dry, without any moisture. We gathered all of them and sorted them out for food and drink. My wife at first cooked the choice herbs for our children, but in time we learned how to spare ourselves that trouble. Our children learned how to eat herbs right from the ground, until the day when they took sick; until that strange Diablik, bearer of evil came into our life.

"Whenever I think of him, of that Diablik, I begin to shake and tremble. How great is my misfortune! He might have been the very cause for their death! I sacrificed both of them to save that Diablik. Heaven forgive me. My little ones might have perished anyway in the forest. Diablik might have been predestined to live, and indeed he has managed to survive to this day. But, who knows. You want me to go on? I gave Diablick whatever dry moldy bread I had left, and when the children became ill with that awful intestinal disease all I had left were herbs.

"We lost the children, both of them in one day, while he, Diablik, remained alive!

"Sometimes I think I am losing my mind. Those awful thoughts keep haunting me all the time. Sometimes, I say to myself, sometimes a very compassionate person is a very cruel person, a totally heartless person. There is compassion that is worse than murder. On whom did I have compassion? On a wild, abandoned child, on a Diablik? I was not the one who brought him to the forest. I did not bear him, I was not responsible for him. But my own children, I brought them with my own arms into the forest, I carried them one by one in a sack on my back, I put them into the pit, they called out to me, 'Father, give us some food! Father, even a crumb! Woe is me for that exchange, but I couldn't leave Diablick to his fate. I found him on a pile of snow in the forest, and how could I help but feel sorry for him? Even a wild animal must have a heart. We lived in the forest on robbery, sometimes even on murder. . . . And yet when I saw Diablik's face I began to tremble. He was lost. It was during the most difficult time of the year, the time of soft snowfall.

The soft carpet of snow kept the marks of our footprints, charting our wanderings during the night. The snow betrayed us, which was why Diablik was forced to move deeper and deeper into the forest, until he came upon our territory. I found him, but he did not want to come with me. He tried to get away. He, who fought daily with the treacherous gentiles did not even trust me, a fellow suffering Jew. 'Who are you and where do you come from?' I asked him. When he got up his courage he told me the peasants called him Diablik, because he would haunt them in the middle of the night like a devil, and they were afraid of him as if he were really an evil spirit. They would throw him slices of bread so that he would not harm them. Horror stories about him circulated in the villages, about the demon who stalks in the night. He, Diablik, knew his power, and how to use it to advantage. He knew how to scare the superstitious peasants, and how to avenge himself on them. He was born in the village, the son of a tailor. The peasants murdered his entire family. They set fire to his house, and the tailor, who was tied to the village and the peasants with thousands of threads, perished along with his wife and children. Only one of his sons, who happened to be playing at the time with the neighbor's children, escaped and hid in the forest. He became the greatly feared Diablik. He knew how to terrorize the peasants by walking about and howling at night, and by playing tricks on the gentiles. He amply deserved his nickname.

"It was very hard to talk him into staying with us in the forest. He did not want to stay in the pit. 'It's too boring,' he said. 'Not to move about at night, not to take revenge of the wicked peasants, not to taunt the German guards, those braggarts who were afraid of their own shadows in the forest . . .' At last he consented to join us. He looked like a devil or an evil spirit. His clothes were ragged, his feet shoeless, his hair grown wild. I found him in the snow, leaning with his back against a trunk of a tree and sleeping peacefully. 'You might have frozen to death in your sleep,' I said. He laughed and said, 'I have a remedy against sleeping too long.' 'What remedy?' 'The lice and fleas in my clothes. They suck my blood and keep waking me up,' Diablik said and laughed. 'Otherwise, I would have died of cold like the last of the Jews who were wandering in the forest last winter.'

"The heat in the pit affected Diablik and he became ill. His was too weak to get up and roam the countryside among the frightened peasants. He lay in the pit shaking with fever. We gave him all our food, our last iron rations which we have saved up for our children. He recovered, but then our children took sick and there was nothing with which to save them. They both died on the same day, and then my wife died. She had no desire to go on living. With her children gone, there was nothing she could wish to live for. Only Diablik and I remained. He called me 'Father,' and each time I heard him say the word my blood would curdle. Father? What kind of a father am I? I am a heartless murderer, not a father. . . .

"I am not sorry, it's a good thing he was saved. If I hadn't rescued him the ravens would be eating his frozen flesh. To this day he calls me Father, and he is very faithful to me. Why is he so faithful to me? What did I do for him that was so special? Any Jew in my place would have done the same thing. I am not sorry, oh no! Heaven forbid . . ."

19

TEN WHO PERISHED AND ONE POOR SOUL
WHO SURVIVED

SOMETIMES one lacks the confidence to retell an extraordinary event which has completely unnerved him. He is afraid people won't believe him. So he tells it as a story told to him by someone else. Not he, but that other person, is responsible for the authenticity of the incident.

This was how one member of the group began to tell his story. He spoke haltingly, unsure of himself. "It's hard to believe," he muttered. Somehow, with everyone opening up, he gathered enough courage to share his own tale. He started with an apology.

"This may sound unreal. You may not believe it, but . . ." Again he grew silent, as if changing his mind and wondering whether he should stop, but presently he reconsidered and went on.

"There was a Jewish *shtetl* in Poland called Vyelun. The Jews called it Vloin. Something happened in that *shtetl* during the first year of the Nazi occupation, on Purim. The Nazi beasts had just begun to show their fangs. The Jews still deluded themselves into thinking that the storm would soon blow over, and that until it did, they could get along with the help of bribes. Bribes, as the Bible says, can even make the wise man blind. . . . In the meantime the preparation for the Purim celebration went on as usual. Still, one could sense that during the reading of the Megilla, the groggers' noise was somewhat restrained. After all, the wicked Haman was alive and well, declaring his intention to 'Destroy, kill and annihilate all the Jews.' And yet, the people of the *shtetl* tried to overlook the threat and wish it away. Some esoteric scholars interpreted the word Haman as an acronym for '*Hitler machar nofel*, Hitler will fall tomorrow. Others maintained that it meant, '*Hitler, Mussolini noflim*, Hitler and Mussolini fall.'

"To befuddle the local lackey of the enemy, the Jews sent him a *shalach manos* of alcoholic beverages so that he would get drunk and not disturb the celebration of Purim. . . .

"What happened on that day defies the imagination. A normal human being with a human brain in his head could not have come up with such a diabolic scheme. Even the victims of that plot thought at first that the fiend was only playing a little joke on them, that he was amusing himself by giving the Jews a good scare . . . He had notified the head of the Jewish community that on Purim day he was going to punish the Jews of the village for having hanged the ten sons of Haman in Shushan, the Persian capital, long ago. Their blood, he claimed, yells at him from the heights of those gallows, and it could only be atoned for by the blood of ten Jews who would be hanged before his eyes in the market place. At first the Jews tried to tell themselves that it was only a joke, which at the very worst would cost them some ransom money. But they came to realize that the villain meant just what he said. Ten Jews, a round *minyan*, were dragged out of their homes as they were about to settle down to their Purim meal, and put in jail.

"The poor souls were captured at random, indiscriminately. Old and young, poor and rich, common folk and higher ups. One of them was a young man who had been married for two days. The fear for the fate of the captured was mixed with a special fear for the fate of the newly wed. The bride nearly lost her mind. And in the middle of the scare, an old man, a neighbor of the groom, went out and announced that he was ready to be hanged in place of the groom. He asked to have the groom set free so that he, the old man, might complete the *minyan*.

"It is hard to believe, but it really happened. I was a witness. I was also involved in the whole thing. It could be that the old man had hoped, as all the Jews in the village did, that the *goy* would call the whole thing off at the last minute. It could also be that he did what he did purposely and deliberately. He was old, well over seventy, old in *mitzvahs* and good deeds, and he might have hoped for the day to come when he could fulfill the *mitzvah* of self sacrifice. He was reputed to have said, 'My life is a handout from the Creator of the World, the Giver of Life. Let Him take it back if He wishes. But this young man, this groom, has his life ahead of him, he still has a great deal to accomplish . . .'

"Who can understand this exchange? Whose mind can comprehend what went through the heart of that groom, whose life was given back to him as a gift by the noble old man? How did it happen that the dim-witted villain agreed to that exchange, to let go of a young man and accept a helpless old man in his place? They say that the villain became confused when he found out that one Jew was prepared to sacrifice his life for another. It was an act of sanctifying the Holy Name publicly. It was said that all those who lived through the Holocaust—the gas chambers and all the other horrors—later related that the awful scene of the hanging of those ten martyrs was more horrible than anything else they had seen or experienced. . . .

"That terrible blow, which struck the Jews on the day of Purim, was greatly softened by the self-sacrifice of that old man, who walked to the gallows happily and joyously. The groom was spared, and he is alive to this day. He survived, but he considered himself more wretched than the ten martyrs who were hanged. Outwardly he remained alive, but inwardly, in his heart, he felt dead. He felt as if every moment of life was given to him in exchange for the life of the old Jew. How could he live freely when his life was not his own? And how could he live in such a way as to deserve the old man's sacrifice? Believe it or not, that groom considered himself unfortunate in the extreme. It could well be that if he had been consulted on the matter he would not have agreed to have that exchange take place. I believe he would have chosen to be hanged. I swear to you he would have chosen to be hanged! I swear to you . . ."

At that moment something exploded. The flow of the story was interrupted by a few voices shouting at the same time,

"It's a lie! You are swearing falsely! How do you know? Stop!" the voices stormed as one voice.

"You will have to believe me! I am that groom! I am the one! The whole thing was done behind my back! Believe me! I have been dead since then, a living dead man! The old man haunts me constantly. He is always demanding that I live a worthy life. And what have I got to offer him? My life is worthless, I swear to you . . ."

His shout overwhelmed the voices of his tense audience, and his voice, the voice of a wounded soul, hushed everyone. He sighed deeply and stopped. . . .

20

RESURRECTION BECAUSE OF A PAIR OF SHOES

"**L**OOK at me and tell me, what am I? A living dead man or a dead live one? Am I as dead as all the other dead, or perhaps I have been resurrected?"

The clown in the group felt that his turn had come to speak up and dispel the dark gloom which had descended upon all the survivors. This fellow thought nothing of joking even at the expense of the most nightmarish memories. Which comes to show that the most somber situation may be a cause for levity. . . .

The clown, seizing upon the opportunity, decided to take advantage of it without any hesitation.

"You may suspect that I am only pulling your leg, or that I am making a fool of myself. But I could bring you an honest to goodness witness who will swear to you that he had dug me a grave and made me one of those happy few who were given a proper Jewish burial. That person told me all about it, and his description of the burial was so convincing that I am inclined to believe that my life since then has been an unfortunate mistake, and that the truth is that I was buried long ago. . . .

"I had come out of my bunker. I didn't walk out, I crawled. I was crawling on all four until I saw sunlight. What can I say? The light was dazzling. Such light had not been seen since the six days of creation. Such brightness! Not ordinary sunlight, but a light that made the sky and air absolutely radiant, and everything was bright and gay. A band was playing in full view in the middle of the street. It was the sound of the band which had drawn me out. I walked slowly up and down the streets. No one followed me, no one called after me *Jude,* and it appeared to me that another Jew was coming towards me, in broad daylight! I stood and yelled out, 'Tuvia!'

"Tuvia turned around, took a look at me, hesitated for a moment, when all of a sudden he turned away and began to run. 'Tuvia, Tuvia!' I yelled as I ran after him. I couldn't overtake him. 'Tuvia, Tuvia!' He ran as fast as an arrow, but I was not about to let him get away. How I was able to run so fast I'll never know. In any case, I overtook him and grabbed him with both hands, not letting go of him. 'Tuvia, Tuvia!' And he, instead of being glad to see me, was shaking all over, his teeth chattering with great fear. 'Go to your rest,' he pleaded, 'go back to your resting place. What do you want from me? I buried you, I didn't harm you. Let go of me!' I was astounded. What was I? A Dibbuk, an evil spirit? And as I stood there, nonplused, Tuvia, my friend in trouble, pried himself loose and ran away. . . .

"And to this day Tuvia has not made peace with the situation. He keeps insisting that he buried me, and even said Kaddish for my soul, as befits a good friend, and he even had my yahrzeit date. . . . How dare I, says he, how dare I doubt all of that? And how can I, who is dead, contradict him, Tuvia, who is alive?

"And how can I really argue with him? He was right there with me in that unspeakable concentration camp, he saw with his own eyes how I was shot and how I dropped dead. He himself had carried me to the burial place and with his own hands he dug the hole. He had risked his life doing it. He could not stand the thought of my body being abused, that I, his good friend, would be eaten up by mice and birds and stray dogs. At night he took a chance and dug me a grave. With his own hands he threw me into the hole, but he did not have a chance to fill it up, because he was frightened away in the middle of doing it. He did what he did according to the laws of Israel. And I, what was I? A demon, an evil spirit? A soul looking for salvation? A soul too restless to remain in the grave? And how can I explain it to Tuvia that I was resurrected, and furthermore, that I owed my resurrection to a pair of shoes, and that the one who had made my resurrection possible was Tuvia himself, who out of respect for me had not taken off my shoes, as was the custom at the time. . . .

"I lay in the grave which Tuvia had dug for me, and the grave, as I have mentioned, had remained open. Shortly after, a corpse thief, one of those brutes who prowled around all the death camps, came across my presumably dead body. Those thieves would go through the clothes of the dead and take whatever struck their fancy. This one took a fancy to my shoes. He tried to pull them off my feet, but was not able to. As he kept pulling, I, the half buried dead man began to yell. I felt as if my legs were being pulled off and I screamed. The thief was terrified. 'You are dead,' he muttered, 'shut up.' He hardly finished saying this when he let go of me and ran away. By now I had completely recovered consciousness. I recalled how I was shot, how I got hit, and how I fell. When I came to, I realized that the bullet had only scratched my ear, and I had fainted from the shock. That thief, by shaking me so much as he tried to pull off my shoes, brought me back to life. Which comes to show that it may pay to leave a dead man's shoes on his feet. . . .

"Since that day, since my resurrection, I have been wondering at myself, what am I? Alive or dead? I am not alive. The reason for living has been taken away from me. I am not dead either, because I remember the moment when I fell down after I was shot. . . .

"Tuvia did not give the whole matter much thought. He did not believe me. He couldn't accept my being alive after he had taken care of my burial, especially since one is commanded by tradition to banish the memory of the dead from one's heart. . . .

"A Jew's luck! Here I am, both alive and dead. After I spoke to Tuvia I found out about my yahrzeit date. On that day I light a yahrzeit candle in my memory, and I say Kaddish for the ascension of my soul, according to our tradition . . ."

21

THE HERO WHO RETURNED THE SLICE OF BREAD

I T was the turn of the *yeshiva bocher*. This fellow had sat by himself during all that time without saying a word, listening intently. He did not take part in the conversation, but kept himself out of the discussions. Only now, after everyone had unburdened himself, the *yeshiva bocher* decided to make his contribution. His voice was carefully measured, his eyes lowered, at times even shut, and he weighed every word before he shared it with the others. . . .

"If we start to count the heroic deeds of individual Jews we may never finish. In fact, why even bother to look for isolated instances of Jewish courage and self-sacrifice? Every hungry Jew was the greatest of heroes! Every day and every moment the hungry Jew who did not forget he was a Jew, was a hero. Hunger can make a person lose his mind and forget his Maker. 'The victims of the sword were better off than the victims of hunger,' the lamenter has said in his lamentation. Does anyone know the meaning of the insanity of hunger better than us, who have experienced it? Does anyone know better than us the longing for a slice of bread?

"As a student of the Talmudic Academy I used to ask myself when I studied the laws of Passover, Why is the Law so strict with the leavened bread, more so than with all other prohibitions? And what is the purpose of the ruling concerning a mere trifle? What is the worth of a crumb that you are commanded to look for it in holes and cracks, and to burn it? There, in the camp, we found out exactly what a crumb of bread meant. We would collect bread crumbs with trembling fingers. Each crumb that stuck to our fingertip we would put on our tongue and swallow with great relish.

"I don't know if any other language in the world has an equivalent to the Hebrew expression *herpat raav,* the disgrace of hunger. You understand, not pain, sorrow, or pangs of hunger. Hunger is also a disgrace. . . . It causes not only physical pain, but it also degrades. It enslaves all of the senses and all of the thoughts, to the point where 'Man is no better than beast.' One dreams of food constantly, whether awake or asleep. One talks about nothing else, and fights over small bits of food with his friends. We used to argue endlessly over the slice of bread which was given to us. One would say, eat it right away, as soon as you get it in the morning, and you will have enough strength to last you until the following day. Another one would say, to the contrary, better keep it until after the hard labor of the day so you will be able to sleep. One maintained that it was best to chew it all at once, while another disagreed, saying that you should suck on every crumb. . . . Our bread had become an involved ritual, a pagan cult!

"But our Sages have maintained, 'Give every person the benefit of the doubt.' Every person includes your own self. . . . To what can this be likened? To a dying oil lamp. You add a few drops of oil, and the flame rises again. So is the soul in a hungry body. Each slice, each crumb, keeps the soul, the Divine Flame, from going out. And as long as the Divine Light burns there is life, hope, faith. Every day of life, even bitter and unhappy life, gave us the hope that we might see the downfall of the wicked.

"Go and learn, how great the faith of the Jews was! Hunger and faith, after all, are opposites! Hunger degrades the soul and makes the body master over it. It puts matter over spirit. But the Jews in the camp knew how to overcome their hunger and remembered that they were Jews. Without a strong faith one would have not been able to keep his bread ration until evening. And many did! I was one of them. The whole thing might have been a matter

114

of conditioning. Only once, only the first time, was difficult. The second time was much easier. It paid to leave the ration. A small piece of bread could save a life. There were some weaker ones among us, who could not save up their ration until evening, and that night they starved, as if they had nothing to eat all day. There were those who shared their bread in the evening with a weak Jew. I did it myself more than once. I didn't look upon it as great sacrifice. What difference did it make? If you were going to die that night, at least you have saved a fellow Jew on your last day. And if not, if you got up in the morning to go to work, you were like a newly born and you had new hope. . . .

"Israel is a holy people! Satan wanted to turn our bread into idol worship, Heaven forbid. But the Jews resisted and prevailed! Here is an incident in which I myself was involved.

"One evening I was summoned by the camp commander. I knew what it meant. Everyone was prepared for this. I immediately settled my account. I made silent confession. I still had my entire bread ration. What use was it now? I said good-bye to my neighbors and divided my worldly possessions among them. This was how we used to do it. I took off my warm coat, and I exchanged my shoes for an old, torn pair. I left, but my luck smiled upon me and I immediately returned. The murderer must have been too lazy to deal with me, and he sent me back to the cabin. I returned listlessly, since I had already made my confession. . . . When I entered the cabin everyone was surprised. They all returned my belongings. I remembered my bread ration. After all, I was alive, and I was still enslaved to that idolatry. . . . My neighbor got up and gave me back my bread. He gave me the whole thing. He didn't even want to keep some for himself. He didn't want to. He returned the entire ration. He was happy I was alive. He was truly happy, you could see it in his face. The courage of a Jew! The moral courage!"

22

RABBI MENDELE OF PABIANITZ GOES TO TREBLINKA

RABBI Mendele of Pabianitz is on his way to Treblinka. He is not walking, he is running. A great multitude of Jews is marching in the deportation parade. Old and young, women with babies in their arms and little ones clinging to the hems of their mothers' dresses, the sick and the crippled, the blind and the lame who lean on their companions. Slowly the crowd moves on, with a faltering pace. The only one who is running is Rabbi Mendele. An ardent will pushes him on, as if all his limbs are feet made for racing. . . .

The armed guards, sneering diabolically, are in no hurry. They are jovial and cheerful. They keep peeking at their watches, as if sorry to see the moments tick away so fast. They want this amusing game to go on and on. They laugh and laugh.

"Ha ha, what's your rush, Jew? Your fate will wait for you . . ."

Rabbi Mendele forges ahead and reaches the front of the procession. His waving beard is competely white except for one black wisp of hair in the middle, like a dark flame. He does not heed the order. He charges forth, as if attempting to sweep all the Jews along with him.

Suddenly something is tossed under his feet and makes him

stumble. A whimper comes from it, a high pitched baby whimper. Rabbi Mendele bends down over the whimpering bundle and raises it with trembling hands. The baby writhes in his arms and a fiendish laughter is heard from the side,

"Hee hee hee, Jew, you won't be in such a hurry now, Jew, hee hee hee—"

Rabbi Mendele carries the writhing whimpering baby in both arms. The squirming infant throws two thin arms around his neck, and Rabbi Mendele runs faster, as if trying to get ahead of the baby's cry. He reaches a dead end, unable to go any further. He is caught in the crowd which is pushing and shoving, milling in one place.

Suddenly Rabbi Mendele feels that his pent up energy shifts from his feet to his brain, and a flood of words comes out of the depths of his soul.

"Do you see, Jews, what I am holding in my hands? This is the sanctum sanctorum, a Jewish baby! Let us consider, dear Jews, how does the sun know it is the sun, and that it brings welfare and blessing? Because evil cannot endure its light, and every time it shines, evil must flee and hide in nooks and crannies! And here is this baby, one of the children of Israel, weak and helpless as a fly, despised and downtrodden like a worm. Why did Satan see fit to enlist all his hosts of destruction, with all their deadly weapons, to wage war against flies and worms? The unholy—the moment they see a Jewish child, a tender little suckling, who hasn't even learned how to say *modeh ani*; the moment they see a Jewish infant in his mother's arms—a murderous passion is kindled in their bosoms. Why? Because the powers of darkness cannot stand the pure and holy looks of Jewish babies and sucklings. Satan has a most refined scent, Heaven help us!

"Believe you me, dear Jews, every single Jew today is lowly and despised in his own eyes. We are a sinful generation, we don't even know how to accept our suffering lovingly. I hereby confess before all of you: When the murderers began to torture me and persecute me I was furious. I almost began, perish the thought, to doubt His justice. . . . But my eyes were soon opened! When the godless beasts discovered a scroll of the Torah in my room, they immediately let go of me and attacked the scroll viciously, with a murderous frenzy.

They stepped on it, they tore it up and shredded the holy parchment. It was as if they sensed that the soul of the Jews was imprinted upon the square letters on the scroll. At that moment I became calm and serene, and I understood the meaning of the verse, 'You have given me greater understanding than my enemies.' It was not I the enemy was after. It was the source of holiness——he was massacring the Jews, he was trying to break the spirit of the Jews by trampling the scrolls of the Torah!

"Oh, Jews! There is a good reason why the worst of all demons has singled us out! Whenever wickedness rears its ugly head it always finds, in every place and in every time, its one enemy, who remains unchanged and irreplaceable, and turns all its fury against him. The devil has always said 'Either the Jew or me!' And today, is it purely an accident that the war is against the Jew? Satan knows his reckoning. He is after the foundation and the root of the world. We can see how true the words of Kuzari are, 'Israel among the nations is like the heart among the parts of the body.' What gives life to the body? The heart. And the forces of purity, morality and justice, where do they come from? From faith in the unity of the Creator, 'Love your brother as yourself,' and the four pillars of the universe, without which mankind cannot exist, as it is written, 'Grace and truth have met, justice and peace have embraced!' And the great consolation of 'And it shall come to pass in the end of days,' where does it come from? All these come from the heart! And which organ immediately senses anything that happens to another organ? The heart! And if the world is afflicted with a calamity, a curse, a plague —who feels it and suffers because of it more than anyone else? The heart! It was King David who said, 'All your waves and your billows passed over me.' And now that the insolence of the devil has grown so great that he has set out to conquer the world, his spear dipped in poison is aimed directly at the heart—the Jewish heart!

"And so I am telling you, my sacred Jews, let us not lose sight of the purpose of this war. Who are we? A link in the chain of the generations. A generation goes and a generation comes, but the war is eternal. Satan in all his wars only has one purpose before his eyes —to wipe out the name of Israel. And look how ancient this war is. It says in the book of Psalms, 'They said, go, and let us destroy them from among the nations and Israel's name no longer will be remembered.' Who can count all the enemies who have arisen against us to destroy us? Their number is equal to the number of the nations. Can we name them all? Edom and Moab, Amalek and Philistia, Senacherib and Nebuchadnezzar, Antiochus and Titus, and the Hamans of all generations from Torquemada to Chmelnitzki and all his offspring. . . . An ancient war it is! And Satan always chooses the mighty ones of the world as his messengers. But what happens to all of them in the end? Our curse is put upon them and their memory is forgotten. Evil does not last for long, for truth grows out of the ground, and falsehood has no leg to stand on. Not a single remnant has remained of the enemies of Israel, may their name perish!"

Rabbi Mendele lifted the trembling, bleeding infant with both hands, the way an open Torah scroll is lifted.

"And this is the Torah. . . . And this is the purpose of the eternal war. The greater the hate against a Jewish infant grows, the greater the cruelty, the more obvious it becomes how abysmal and horrible the corruption of the enemy is, bearing the seeds of his destruction. Satan has risen before our eyes, determined to destroy everything, to smother every holy spark, to annihilate all that is pure and good. And so his hatred for the household of Israel is as strong as death, and his thirst for blood is unquenchable. Behold and see, even when he thinks he has conquered the whole world, Satan is seized with fear and trembling when a Jewish child looks at him. And even if the entire world should crumble under the burden of evil, there will yet appear on the debris of the world one last Jew, one single Jew, who will destroy the reign of the devil and will emerge victorious."

Rabbi Mendele had yet much more to say, but the words no longer came out. His voice became a sweet song which flooded his soul. He shook and trembled with the song from the tips of his fingernails to the tips of his toes, and was swept on the waves of a mighty river, carried away when . . . when a murderous hand pulled him by his beard and stopped the song inside of him.

"Ha-ha-ha, you are the Jew with the most beautiful beard, you will lead the procession on its last journey. Fast!"

Rabbi Mendele came back to himself. He turned his face and his beard to his fellow Jews and the hidden song burst out.

"Listen, my brothers, do you know where we are going? We are going on the ancient road of martyrdom, of *kiddush ha'shem.* Our father Abraham took Isaac to be sacrificed and they went joyously and ecstatically. 'And they went together,' which means, they went joyously. What about us? We are going together to our sacrificial altar, fathers and sons, grandchildren, mothers and grandmothers, entire families, heads of the community—what a great moment this is! Stop and think, my dear Jews, my pure and holy Jews, why are we being taken to the slaughter? Satan himself has told us why. Because our name is Israel. We are going to sanctify the name. Slow down, Jews, rest awhile. These are our last moments. Let us fulfill the mitzvah of giving up our life for the sanctification of God's name with our whole heart.

"Here I am, ready and willing to give up my flesh and bones, my blood and my soul, to die the four different kinds of death and to undergo all the tortures . . ."

A deep silence descended upon everybody. All eyes were riveted upon the fiery face of Rabbi Mendele, and a sense of deliverance prevailed.

The silence was interrupted by the soft, fatherly voice of Rabbi Mendele, who spoke slowly.

"Anyone who brings me water to wash my hands before uttering my confession will receive half of my portion in the world to come."

23

THE STORY OF A JEW WHO DEFEATED
THE ANGEL OF DEATH

IT happened on the fourteenth of Nissan, on the eve of Passover. Until that day I was almost able to make peace between me and that angel who is all eyes, known as the Angel of Death. During the early days he never stopped badgering me, making my life miserable. "Hey, listen, you, I am coming to collect the debt you owe me." When I tried to throw that debt in his face, "Here, take this heap of bones and leave me alone!" he rolled with a demonic laughter, "Hee hee, don't you know how merciful I am? I collect my debt penny by penny, with the highest interest. You will pay with tears and blood, because I am so merciful . . ."

When I realized how "merciful" he was, I began to plead with him. I even went so far as to shed tears in front of him. "Please, my good man, I do not deserve all the kindness you are showing me. If I am doomed to die, let me die once and for all. But to die a thousand deaths, to see my doom before my eyes and never know whether this is really the end or whether you are just having yourself some fun—no, sir. How can I confess a thousand times? Surely to do this is to show disrespect to you! . . ."

When he heard me say the word "fun" he burst into a laughter which shook his whole body. "Hee hee, you've hit the nail right on the head. Really, all I am doing is having some fun . . ." He stopped in the middle of the sentence, as if hit by lightning. What a strange creature! Was he sorry he had disclosed his secret? Or did my face reveal my decision to resist him? At that moment he resorted to his typical slyness. "So, you seem to have grasped the rules of my game. I will have you know I do not play with smart alecs who catch on to me . . ." He spoke gravely, and went on slowly, as if counting coins. "Look here, I am willing to let go of you completely, not tease you and not torture, you, but only on one condition—" I couldn't contain myself and I cut him short, "Tell me what it is, come to the point!" He went on: "My condition is that from now on you are mine, completely mine! You may go wherever you want and even believe you are alive, and you may make others believe you are alive. But you must forget completely the cycle of time. From now on you have no days and no weeks, no weekdays and no Sabbath, no holiday and no festival. Time no longer exists for you!"

I accepted his condition. I was forced to accept. I was doomed anyway. The Angel of Death was watching me constantly with his myriad eyes, eating my flesh ceaselessly right off my body. . . . "I am your sole property in any case," I sighed. And at that very moment I lost all concept of time. My inner life had left me, and I was left an empty vessel. The Angel of Death was now my close friend and companion. He spoke to me kindly and amiably, and even tried to enlist me to his service, like all those others. . . . But in the middle of all this a crisis occurred. The big-bellied German, the most faithful assistant of the devil, asked, "Does any of you know when Pesach is?" No one had sought to find out whether a Jewish calendar still existed. No one had asked, we wouldn't have dared ask. But apparently the German had kept a Jewish calendar himself. That same morning he brought us the good news, "You may like to know, you damned Jews, that tonight is Pesach. In honor of your holiday I will roll your bones a bit, the way you used to roll those skinny matzos of yours."

And here is where the story begins. Pesach. Forgotten concepts and customs came rushing back into my empty brain. They stirred and resuscitated my memory, awakening my dormant sense of time. "Today is Pesach?" a flickering flame, hidden deep down inside me, flared up and set my mind on fire. All the memories of the last days of Pesach which I had spent in the ghetto came rushing through my head. Each time the hope to have some matzo seemed to die, a miracle occurred at the last moment and we found some matzo for the holiday. But now? Now? What will happen now? I knew that by merely thinking of "now" I broke my covenant with the Angel of Death. . . . All the memories which had tied me to the living world began to flood my mind, and I knew beyond a doubt that to-night a miracle was going to happen. I didn't know how—but at that moment I was ready to swear that here in the death camp, in-side the kingdom of the Angel of Death I was going to taste the flavor of Pesach. And the miracle occurred, that same day, at twi-light. . . .

When we came back from the back-breaking work at the bon-fires in which the bodies of the gas chamber victims were burned; we used to see peasants milling about on the other side of the elec-trified barbed wires fences. Behind the screen of thick black smoke which arose from the bonfires, the peasants used to do a brisk trade with the doomed Jews inside. This trade was quick as lightning. The peasants would deftly stick their calloused hands between the electrified wires holding out an onion, a potato, or a raddish, and in exchange the peasant would receive a gold coin, a diamond, or some other valuable. The peasants in the vicinity knew that the Jews inside the death camp hid many valuables in their clothes, and were willing to risk their lives to do some "business." As for us, we had nothing to lose. . . . That day I discovered a gold coin in the lapel of a worn out *capote*, and on my way to the cabin in the dark my luck smiled upon me and I discerned a hand between the barbed wires holding out yellow grains of wheat. The peasant must have been quite surprised to receive my gold coin in exchange for the wheat, for his hand trembled. He did not realize what a treasure he had given me, or that it was I who had received the better of the deal. My eyes lit up when I saw the wheat—the miracle had come to pass. Out of these grains I was going to make a matzo for the holiday. . . .

All the way back to the cabin I was trembling with a joy I had never known before. Inside the cabin it was dark as usual. An oppressive fear pervaded. Everyone knew it was the night of the first Seder. Everyone knew that something ominous was about to happen. We were forced back into the cabin earlier than usual, and we were told to go to sleep on our hard wooden bunks. My good luck continued—I was appointed night watchman in my cabin. I paced the cabin floor and I knew that tonight the world was mine. I used two bricks as millstones. I put the grains between the bricks and ground them into a powder which I called flour. I quickly mixed the flour in some water and made some kind of dough for baking matzos. I made a fire in the small iron stove. I used a chair for firewood, and on the red hot stove I baked some kind of a matzo cake the like of which the world has never seen. But who in the entire universe could be compared to a Jew who managed to bake a matzo in total defiance of the Angel of Death and his henchmen?

I was absorbed in my fantasies, enjoying the sweet thoughts of how I was going to celebrate the Seder in the dark cabin, when the alarm siren began to whine. A siren in the middle of the night? It was no doubt a siren in honor of the holiday, the Feast of Freedom. . . . Half naked we all ran out. The big-bellied German began blurting out his orders. "Fall down! Get up! Fall down! Get up! Lie down!" As I lay flat on my belly in the mud I could only think of the bread of affliction which I had baked, and it occurred to me that the mud puddle I was lying in was my Seder couch. . . . As I was lying there I closed my eyes and said the *shehecheyanu*, and I began to chew my little bit of a matzo, which was as hard as rock. But so contented was I as I lay, that I fell asleep.

I still remember that sleep. I clearly remember how I was shaken out of that heavenly rest by a pair of military boots ramming at my ribs. I felt one boot scratching the skin off my face while the other boot was reducing my stomach to a pulp. "You feel good, hey, you filthy Jew?" I heard a cry of rebuke mixed with a raucous laughter, and I immediately recognized the voice of my old friend. "Hee hee, answer me, you, Jew bastard!" He kept grinning. But what did I have to say? I clenched my teeth, and I suffered without saying a word. "Scream, Jew!" he burst out and began to kick me with both feet, but I did not say a word.

My outward silence made me scream silently inside. To stop

my inner screaming I knew I had to overcome my pain and accept my suffering lovingly. Do you really think that suffering is always bitter and painful? Far from it. If you can push your suffering deep down into the ground of your being, you begin to taste a new feeling, which is sweeter than honey. You begin to feel the supreme warmth which surrounds that suffering, and you begin to taste the joy which consumes your soul. . . .

At that moment I heard a wild roar, full of despair, coming not from the fat-bellied German, but from the Angel of Death himself. "Scream, stubborn Jew, scream, or this will be the end of you!" Around and above me I heard the flapping of his black wings, I felt his breath on my face, his knife flashed before my eyes—he had finally come to collect his debt. But I lay there still and quiet. I knew that my revenge was contained in the little bit of matzo inside of me. When that demon riveted his myriad furious eyes upon me I smiled derisively right into his face. He couldn't stand that smile. He took off, and I haven't seen him since. . . .

24

THE THREE DAYS OF TESHUVA OF THE JEWS
OF DZIALOSHITZ

HAVE you ever heard of the holy community of Dzialoshitz?
It was located in the province of Pinchov, not far from the town of
Michov, between Skalimir and Weisslitz. Not too many people have.

It was a quiet community which made no waves in the world.
In that community, one of the 950 Jewish communities of Poland,
there was an ancient synagogue made of wood, an old rabbi, and a
centuries-old cemetery with a shack over the grave of an anonymous
holy man. The Jews of Dzialoshitz used to visit the grave of that
holy man to present their pleas and to beseech him to help them
avert any future trouble. The community thus went about its business quietly and peaceful, like a primordial stream making its way
among the dense trees in some faraway forest. . . .

But the fateful day arrived, and the hand of the destructive
demon reached this quiet and forgotten corner of Polish Jewry. The
deportation decree which was issued against all the Jewish communities of Poland did not elude the Jews of Dzialoshitz. The entire Jewish community was ordered to prepare for the deportation
journey which was to depart from the central market place at noon,
three days later.

When the decree was made known, panic took hold of the town. The Jews began to discuss their plight among themselves, looking for a way to deal with it.

Some said: "All hope is not yet lost. We will prepare food, and even if we have a long way to go, we will endure it and with God's help we will survive."

Others said: "All is lost. We are being sent to our doom. We will never come back."

"Don't give the devil any ideas," the first ones scolded them. "Let's look at the decree. It says that everyone is allowed to take along 25 kilograms in luggage. We must make sure to take along the most necessary items. Food, pillows and blankets for the little ones, and also a kettle for making tea. This should suffice until we reach a resting place. So you see, the decree is not so harsh, all hope is not yet lost, Heaven forbid."

"You cannot rely on the decree," the more pessimistic ones retorted. "The whole thing is contrived to blind us to the truth. Our fate is sealed. We are being led like sheep to the slaughter. It is sad to see condemned people worrying about trivial things to the last minute."

"So, in your opinion, what should we do? What is left for us to do?"

"What a question! In such a terrible and fearful time all we can do is repent and do *teshuva.*"

Teshuva! The echo of the word still reverberated in the air when a great light, a divine light, began to illumine the recesses of their hearts.

Who had brought that word out of the secrecy of his soul?

Was it Shimon, the old *melamed,* who had taught many of the people of the community, or was it that cripple, the son of Rabbi Kalman the *dayan?* That boy was known to be a *zaddik,* and rumor had it that he was a *lamed vavnik.*

The signal was given, and everyone clung to it, like a drowning man clinging to a straw. Even the desperate ones clung to it, along with those who still hoped for a miracle.

Shimon, the old *melamed,* in whom a spark of hope still flickered, began saying,

"My friends, let us have mercy upon ourselves and upon the

future generations. Let us do *teshuva* like the sinful people of Nineveh, and by virtue of our *teshuva* we will avert the evil decree. Let us each pray for the rescue of his family and friends, so that we may have a memory left after we are gone."

And the cripple, the son of the *dayan,* turned to the desperate ones and said,

"Jews! Let us not waste such a great moment with vain thoughts. In three days we will all be called upon to offer ourselves for the Sanctification of the Holy Name. Let us accept the Judgment. The gates of mercy may be closed, but the gates of *teshuva* are always open to us. Let us all do perfect *teshuva* so that we may join the high rung of those who sanctify His name from everlasting to everlasting!"

And so the three days of horror of the holy community of Dzialoshitz became three days of *teshuva* and spiritual uplifting.

With fervor and holy devotion the Jews congregated, young and old, women and children, at the synagogue. The holy ark was opened, and amid the blasts of the shofar three days of public fast were announced, to be observed by everyone, from the youngest to the oldest.

From the synagogue they all went to the old cemetery. They prostrated themselves upon the graves, especially upon the grave of that anonymous holy man, and their praying and wailing pierced the heavens.

As they cried and wailed a voice was heard from among the graves. It was the voice of the cripple, the son of the *dayan.*

"Holy Jews! There is no *teshuva* without confession and repentance. Let us each confess his sins and the Lord of Heaven will forgive us. Our rabbis have taught that even the Day of Atonement does not atone for sins between man and man, until such time when one has forgiven and received forgiveness from his fellow man. Let us ask one another for forgiveness, lest we might have sinned against one another in deed or in thought. Let us repent of the evil and the Lord of Heaven will forgive us and we will be prepared to welcome the Divine Presence."

The public confession began.

The cripple read the confession out loud and the congregation repeated after him word for word,

128

"For the sin which we have sinned before You . . ."

All hearts were united, all souls became one. No one prayed for personal rescue and salvation. Their worldly considerations had disappeared, and their souls were distilled and clung to the Father above.

At the end of the confession, Shimon, the old *melamed*, gathered around him all his offspring and spoke to them as follows:

"Hear my words, my sons and daughters, my grandsons and granddaughters, my great-grandsons and my great-granddaughters. Our Sages of blessed memory have taught, 'Even if a sharp sword is resting on a man's neck, let him not despair of mercy.' The mercy of Heaven is great, like the mercy of a father for his children. If the decree is irreversible, let us ask for mercy for our souls, so that we may sanctify His blessed Name. Thus the biblical verse, 'The loving and the pleasant, in their life and in their death they were not separated,' will be fulfilled in us, and our souls will be bound forever in the bonds of eternal life, along with the souls of all the righteous who sacrificed life for the Sanctification of His Name!"

At dawn of the third day of *teshuva* and fasting, all the men of Dzialoshitz gathered in the old shul, they and their wives and children. They all wore their Sabbath clothes, wrapped in kittls, as they did each year on Yom Kippur, and they prayed *neila*. "You extend Your hand to the transgressors and Your right hand is open to receive those who do *teshuva* . . ." They made a public confession: "We are guilty, we have betrayed, we have robbed, we have slandered . . ." Afterwards they blew the shofar and called out seven times, "The Lord—He is God!"

At the end of the heart-rending prayer it was time to gather at the market square. Deep silence overcame the people in the synagogue—a terrible and lofty silence. The cripple made his way to the holy ark to say good-bye to the old shul, in which many generations of Jews forged the chain of Torah and tradition.

"Jews, sons of Abraham, Isaac and Jacob! The three days of *teshuva* were only a preparation for the great and terrible day of judgment which is upon us. With the consent of the Omnipresent One, with the consent of the entire holy congregation, and with the consent of all the generations before us, we swear to be strong and to strengthen one another in our holy faith until our last breath of life! May it be His will that for the sake of our fathers and for the sake of little children we will deserve to see our soul depart from our body as we utter the word ONE. Hear O Israel, the Lord is our God, the Lord is ONE!"

The deportation began. A procession of pale faced Jews, Jews who had just prayed *neila,* Jews who had forgotten all worldly considerations because of the long fast, Jews with wings. . . .

From all sides of the market place of Dzialoshitz a multitude of gentiles, the peasants from the neighboring villages, the neighbors of the Jews for so many generations, gathered, axes stuck in their belts, and bags on their shoulder, waiting like vultures to begin their looting. The procession moved on, and it seemed that a human spark was awakened in the gentiles. Somehow they were touched by the solemn sight of Jews marching in their Sabbath finery down the eternal path of martyrdom.

"Ola boga! Tzo za shviento? Yak na orichistoshtz! Ola boga!" (Heavenly Father! What holiday is this for the Jews? Seems like a great holiday for them! Heavenly Father!) the elderly gentiles were saying in great surprise.

The marching Jews did not look back, they heard nothing and saw nothing. They marched festively, their hearts yearning for the hoped-for shore. . . .

So it was that the holy community of Dzialoshitz, one of the 950 Jewish communities of Poland, embarked on its last journey. . . .

25

HOW RABBI SHEM OF CRACOW WON A VICTORY
OVER HIMSELF

ALL his life Rabbi Shem of Cracow strove to fulfill the commandment, "Love your neighbor as yourself," in all its simplicity and wholeness, but he was never able to do so. Whenever his Hasidim silently entered his special room, he repeated to himself with great humility the three words, *veahavta-lereacha-kamocha,* you shall love your neighbor as yourself. And although he struggled all his days to efface himself completely before all the Jews who knocked at his door, although he would rush over to them with a merciful heart, with open arms, and with eyes flowing with great love—he was not satisfied.

Rabbi Shem entered the Pardes, the orchard of the Torah with all its secrets and mystic love and those three words—*veahavta lereacha kamocha,* shone before him with all the colors of the rainbow. The words took on the veil of *Sod,* the secret, mystic meaning. *Reacha,* your neighbor, is the Holy One Blessed Be He, as it is written, "Your neighbor and your father's neighbor do not forsake . . ." The words beckoned to him with the *Remez,* the biblical allusion. *Rea* is a derivation from the root *raah,* evil, and the allusion is to accepting lovingly the good and the evil together. . . . The words took on the adornment of the *Drash,* the allegorical expounding. *Veahavta — kamocha,* and you shall love — like yourself. What does "yourself" mean? Was there a commandment among the 613 commandments concerning loving oneself? Indeed there was a commandment "And you shall be careful to guard yourselves." Which meant, that the Jewish soul within oneself needed to be guarded and loved, and it was from there that we derived the command, "Your neighbor as yourself". . .

But Rabbi Shem did not stop there. He demanded of himself more and more.

"But still, the biblical text must be understood in its *Pshat,* in its literal meaning. And how does one achieve this commandment in its literal meaning, with all its strictness? "Love your neighbor as yourself." As yourself! That is to say, with all the innocence you can find in yourself, without any special effort, without any special reasons and motives, every moment, without taking your mind off of it, just as you love yourself and no one else.

"What is the use," the Rabbi would criticize himself, "what is the use of having a Jew help a Jew like himself, if when he does it he sees himself as the "giver" and the other as the "receiver"? And what is the use if at the time when I lower my head and look with love and friendship at the face of every Jew, I see the difference between my silken garments and his simple *kapote?*"

Thirty-five years Rabbi Shem led his congregation, and he was still searching for the full meaning of that commandment, until the opportunity arrived in that hell on earth called Kazet. To humiliate the Jews, a Kazet was set up in the ancient cemetery of Cracow, known to the Polish populace as Jerusalem Street.

Here, in this awful jail, Rabbi Shem saw himself freed at last from the prison of his body and his worldliness. His tormentors, those demons of destruction, kept torturing his body with every device at their disposal, but they were only able to harm his outer shell, his physical being. And the more that outer shell shrivelled and shrunk and lost its presumed worth, the more his inner core, over which the devil had no dominion, would reveal its true nature.

What did he care about the devil and his minions? The frail and submissive body was being beaten, but it was like the beating of wheat for the purpose of taking out the grain. The longer you beat on it the more chaff fell off and the more pure the grain that was left.

All his life Rabbi Shem had been engaged in a desperate battle between his outer shell and his inner core; between his dead being— the part that came from dust and would return to dust—and his living being—the divine essence emanating from the source of all life, drawing constantly from that source and aspiring back to it all the time. Here, in this hell on earth, each day his body was being destroyed, but the holy Rabbi was at peace. The battle was over. The body had lost, and the soul was celebrating its victory.

Now, as his physical powers were ebbing, Rabbi Shem began to grasp the true meaning of the commandment "Love your neighbor as yourself" in all its simplicity. He no longer felt his own personal pain. He only felt the pain of the Jews around him. Their pain was his pain. The pain of every Jew in this hell made his whole body ache. But what was he to do for the pain and sorrow of all the Jews?

"What have you got to tell us, our master and teacher?" the eyes of all the suffering Jews asked him, screaming soundlessly. And it was this inner, spiritual scream that went right through his very being, making every limb and cell in his body tremble.

"*Gevalt!* The Lord help me!" Rabbi Shem's scream welled up in his heart, the scream of a purged soul.

"Have mercy on us, our master! We have mercy on you, our master, have mercy upon us!" the Jews pleaded knocking on the closed gates of divine mercy. They pleaded without voice. Only an occasional groan was heard, followed by silence. Each groan of each Jew filled Rabbi Shem's entire being, as if it came from his own heart.

"*Gevalt!* I can no longer remain silent! I just can't!" Rabbi Shem's sigh shook heaven and earth.

Things were getting worse. The tortures were intensified, and the situation became unbearable. Without a word, they all clung to Rabbi Shem, who dwelled among them in the depths of their agony. They clung to him as a bandage clings to an open wound. And the martyrized Rabbi whose battered and broken limbs no longer separated him from the rest, began to gag on his followers' unbearable pain. He then opened his mouth, not to console them, but to console himself.

"What can I say, my fellow Jews? You want me to tell you how I am able to bear this burden? Very simple, friends. Each morning when I say the blessing, 'Who did not create me a gentile,' a miraculous power is renewed within me to bear everything. Never before did I utter this blessing with my whole being, for I did not know exactly what 'gentile' meant. Truly, now we Jews know full well why we have to thank and praise and extol the Almighty for 'Not having made us like the gentiles, or like the families of the earth, not having given us a portion like theirs, and not having cast our lot with all their multitude.' I need not console you, my dear friends. The blessing 'Who did not create me a gentile' should be sufficient to comfort every suffering Jew!"

"Let us consider the matter," Rabbi Shem grew excited and began to stand up on his shaky feet. It was not his own strength enabling him to stand, but the strength of the Jews around him, who were animated by his words. :"I have a serious question to ask you, my dear Jews! Think about it carefully before you answer it. I ask you, who of you would be willing to trade his share in this world, yes, yes, in this world, for the share of these accursed villains, whose good fortune is smiling upon them at this moment? If each of us were given the choice at this moment to be the victim or the victimizer, what would he choose, even here, in this hell? Who would dare stand up and say, that he is envious of the lowly murderers and would like to be like one of them? By all means, let him get up and say so, Who?"

A hush fell upon the listeners. No one spoke.

Rabbi Shem felt the heart beats of the Jews in his own heart, and he went on.

"*Gevalt!* Master of the Universe! Is there one Jew who would like You to turn him into a murderous gentile?"

"Rabbi, Rabbi, I swear to you on the memory of my holy mother, even I wouldn't want it."

The voice, which cut the silence in the darkened cabin, came from the corner of the room near the door. That voice, hoarse with shouting, was well known. It was the voice of the only Jewish Capo in that torture camp.

134

"You must believe me this time, my fellow Jews! I swear by the memory of my holy mother!" the Capo yelled. "Rabbi! Rabbi! You at least must believe me! At least you! I serve the murderers, and I must know what they are like!"

The Capo seemed to have been startled by his own strange outburst, and without further ado he left the cabin.

"Heavenly Father! I believe, even him I believe. I believe him when he says he does not want to become one of the murderous gentiles, who suck the blood of the Jews."

Rabbi Shem sighed and all the Jews sighed along with him.

The noose was further tightened around the necks of the Jews. A tremor kept running through Rabbi Shem's heart. He saw Jews crying all around him. They cried without stop.

"The fountain of tears is meant to purify and purge the soul," the Rabbi tried to relieve the pain of the weeping Jews, and as he spoke he felt tears choking in his throat. "We must not waste our pure tears on bodily pain."

"Rabbi, Rabbi, it is not for our own selves that we are crying. The Capo had told us that the order was given . . ."

Rabbi Shem knew that his time had come.

He felt wholeness in his soul, as if "All my bones will utter, Lord, who is like You?" The body and the soul had made peace between themselves, reaching the rung of "You will be whole with the Lord your God." And from the wholeness of deed and of thought there is only one step to the ecstasy of the soul.

"God help us all!" the Rabbi heard the moaning of the Jews who were fearful for his fate, and their pain and humiliation began to weigh upon him.

Rabbi Shem started on his last journey while two feelings warred inside of him. A feeling of great yearning, lifting him up on the wings of eagles to join the martyrs of all generations; and a feeling of deep sorrow, pulling him down and binding him with bonds of suffering to those who were forced by Satan to gather together and witness the fate of their teacher and master.

He struggled with himself, chasing away all lofty and noble feelings which lifted him upward. He folded his wings, which kept growing larger and larger, lowered himself down and strained to commune fully and totally with the suffering Jews around him. He realized he was naked, and that his Jewish brothers were ashamed for him. He raised his eyes and with a voice not his he called out to the henchmen who were preparing to do their work.

"My last wish is to have my small prayer shawl to be able to say my confession."

"Jewish impudence!" the chief executioner barked.

"My commander, sir, I humbly ask to grant him his wish!" It was the hoarse voice of the Jewish Capo, who accompanied the chief executioner.

"Shut your mouth, your dirty Jew! If you don't stay out of this I will put you right there with your Rabbi!"

Suddenly he changed his mind. It could be that he wanted to prolong the death throes of the condemned Rabbi. He said,

"I order you to fulfill his last wish."

"Officer, sir, I humbly request to be permitted to carry out your order," the Capo spoke again.

"It's your job, Capo," the executioner blurted at him.

Rabbi Shem took the tallis from the Capo's trembling hands. He wrapped himself in it and for a moment he stood there hesitating. It was time to confess, but to whom should he direct his words, to the One above or to those below? And how could he use his confession to somehow assuage the pain of his fellow Jews?

He braced himself, looked around at the Jews and felt his love for them as a pure *kamocha,* "as yourself," without a blemish or a reservation. At that moment he lifted his eyes to heaven and cried out with a powerful voice,

"May it be Your will, that I may become the atonement for all the Jews!"

The muffled echo of bullets. . . .

Rabbi Shem shook and quivered. Through a lightning he saw the shining eyes of the gathered Jews brimming with tears. He began to fly, the useless shell in the form of a body was shed, like leaves in autumn, and he flew higher and higher, like one who had won a victory over himself.

26

THE NINETEEN DAY JOURNEY OF DEATH

"OF all the unspeakable forms of death which the Nazi beasts had invented to exterminate the Jews, the worst of all was death by hunger and asphyxiation in the boxcars of the death trains. Why was it so awful? Because it came after long days and nights of protracted agony, and because one saw his friends die and could do nothing to help. Worse yet, one felt as if his friends took up his own space and breathed his own air, and whenever one of them was gone, he would feel relieved. He would proceed to stand up on his faltering feet, enlarge his territory, and breathe more freely . . ."

These are the words of Pinchas'l, a survivor of Buchenwald and Mauthausen.

Pinchas'l had spent nineteen days in the death train. During his journey he had reached the conclusion that anyone who said that the body sustained the soul was mistaken. It was the other way around. And the proof for this came at the end of the death journey, when even Bogush had to agree with Pinchas'l's conclusion and admit that his Jewish fellow-sufferer was right.

Bogush was Pinchas'l's Capo. He was the ruthless overseer of the

Jewish prisoners in the secret factory which manufactured the Panzer Faust.

Pinchas'l was surprised to find out that his listener had never heard about the Panzer Faust.

"This Nazi weapon was born in the last phase of the war," Pinchas'l explained. "Panzer Faust literally means an armored fist. It was a hand weapon designed for desperate street fighting against armor and tanks. It was an ordinary iron pipe filled at one end with powerful explosives. The explosives were an odd mixture of dark powder, dynamite, some brown powder, trotil, and a sprinkling of white powder resembling sugar. Some prisoners were tempted to taste the mixture and they died within minutes. . . . They were the lucky ones! The rest were being poisoned slowly. The poisonous powder entered their lungs and their flesh turned brown, like trotil. . . .

The able bodied ones, who managed to stay alive, were told one clear day to enter the boxcars of a death train. Twelve hundred men were taken to the Flisburg torture camp near Leipzig. They were all crammed into nine narrow and closed boxcars, some one hundred-forty men in each car. . . .

Pinchas'l found himself in the same boxcar with Bogush, the Capo. Bogush was a prisoner himself, and his life was uncertain. He wore a triangular green patch on his chest, which marked him as a political prisoner. Criminals wore black or red triangles. Bogush was Polish. The Germans had suspected him of collaborating with the Polish underground. But as soon as he became Capo in charge of the Jewish prisoners, Bogush began to persecute them, outdoing his German masters whom he hated.

"Two souls are struggling inside that gentile," Pinchas'l used to say, as he grappled with the mystery of it. "On the one hand he faithfully serves the German murderers and fawns before them like a dog. He undoubtedly senses that their demented hatred for the Jews surpasses their hatred for the Polish rebels, and he, Bogush, sings them songs of praise and wishes them success and victory. . . . On the other hand he shows at times a bottomless hatred for the German tyrants who oppress him and his fellow countrymen, and when they are not around to listen he curses them and damns them." At such time Bogush would turn to the suffering Pinchas'l and plead before him, "Please, you are a pious Jew, pray to God that the downfall of the Germans should not be long in coming! . . ."

There was no doubt in Pinchas'l heart that this gentile had become attached to him because he knew that Pinchas'l's faith was as strong as granite, and because Pinchas'l believed without any doubt that wickedness was about to disappear, and the Germans would be crushed underfoot. Because of this faith Bogus respected him and tried to mitigate his inhuman ordeals as much as he could. . . . But Bogush's tokens of friendship repelled Pinchas'l whenever he saw how Bogush tormented the rest of the Jews. Once Pinchas'l got up his courage and told Bogush,

"A gentile is always a gentile! Esau will always remain Esau! The damned Germans, even on the threshold of hell, in the face of their defeat, are not able to forget for a moment their hatred for the Jews! And you, Pollaks, are no better! Your hatred for the Jews has made you lose your mind, it made you collaborate with the Germans, and now you are trapped!"

"A Zhid is always a Zhid! Whoever was born a Zhid, will remain a Zhid!" Bogush retorted frankly, with a tinge of irony. "The Jew, even when he is beaten up, stepped on, pulled apart limb from limb, even when his whole body is burning, he continues to hold on to his faith. His soul is squeezed out of his body, and his lips utter a prayer to his God . . ."

Now, having been thrown together in the same boxcar, the discussion between them was renewed with greater fervor.

"So you see, Bogush, all your cruelty hasn't done you one bit of good! Your end is like the end of all the tortured Jews!" Pinchas'l told Bogush, not to taunt him, but merely to make him think and repent of what he had done.

"No, sir. Even here, in the death train, I rule, and your lives are in my hands! Even here, in the common grave of those who are buried alive, the struggle continues, and the strong is bound to win!" Bogush smiled a triumphant smile. And to substantiate his words he clenched his fist and hissed between his teeth, "Panzer Faust". . . .

And this is how the discussion, which was to last nineteen days, for the duration of the entire journey, began. . . .

✻ ✻ ✻

On the first day of the journey the death train began to roll. The live cargo in the boxcars did not budge. The mass of passengers was petrified in a nightmarish stupor. Under the deluge of blows delivered by the whizzing crops, the human shadows were reduced to a faceless pulp. Each heap of dry bones which was thrown into the suffocating boxcar lost all desire to go on living, and thoughts of individual identity disappeared. It was as if limbs were no longer personal or private, but were scattered about, and all bodies became one indistinguishable mass. . . .

What became of Pinchas'l inside the train? He was one of the human splinters lost in the congealed, frozen mass, without any will or purpose. What did he do at that time? He let go of his body, letting his limbs spread out as the space and the air permitted, and somehow he strove to keep his mind working. His mind dove into an abysmal state of stupefaction. At the bottom of the abyss everything was clear and translucent like a dream. In his dream he saw his father and mother, his brothers and sisters, his oldest brother, Yehezkel Nathan, with his seven children. The youngest, what's his name. . . . He was ashamed in his dream not to remember his nephew's name. . . . Oh, yes, sweet Moishe'le!

Moishe'le stands next to his mother's death bed. The bed is outside in the yard, under the open sky, in public view. The "Selection" has just taken place. Moishe'le's father, Yehezkel Nathan, and his six uncles are standing on the other side, ready for the deportation. His mother, Leah Gnendil, lies in bed, waiting for a German bullet to end her life. Sweet Moishe'le clings to his mother like to dear life. He won't leave her. He'd rather die with her. . . . Pinchas'l hears himself crying in his dream. He is crying with shame and sorrow, with regret and anguish. Why did he leave his own mother in the Stopnitz Ghetto? It would have been much better to have clung to her and die along with her. It was father's fault! His old father had told him, "Go away, Pinchas'l, run away and hide! Go wherever you can! God willing, you may live to be my last Kaddish."

Pinchas'l was caught in the web of the dream. Meanwhile the frozen mass began to separate and wake up. He woke with a shiver and became a splinter once again. Bogush the Capo began to distribute some food rations to the prisoners on the death train. The mass was now completely separated, each little piece struggling for its own self-preservation. Only Pinchas'l, still lost in his dream, remained inactive. Bogush noticed him. He pulled him up by his hair and yelled in his ears,

"Panzer Faust!"

What he meant was, Get up and fight with your teeth and nails for your right to live! Rise and use all your remaining strength in the war of survival!

Pinchas'l, in whose mind his father's plea to run for his life still echoed, did not grasp Bogush's simple words, and he responded out of his dream,

"God willing!"

❖ ❖ ❖

By the third day of the journey the refuse stench inside the boxcar had became unbearable. Some of the people inside had suffocated and died. Since fewer people were now breathing, it became less stifling. The corpses still took up space, but they had been placed on the bottom section. The stronger men took the upper section, while the dead and the dying remained below. Thus, the ones below became a footstool for the ones above.

Pinchas'l was struggling to stay apart from both—the ones above and the ones below. He was growing weaker, his knees were beginning to give way. If he were to take a seat among the ones above he would feel better, but he could not bring himself to desecrate the dead, let alone harm the dying. . . . At times he would reprimand himself: Why is your mind so lucid and alert? Why isn't your heart hardened and insensitive like all the rest? One thought filled his head: Not to become, God forbid, a murderer in his last days. For he who robs a dying man of one breath is a murderer. The accursed Germans, the sons of the devil, would throw in small pieces of bread through the single small window in the boxcar, inciting the doomed prisoners to fight one another. More than once did a prisoner snatch a mouldy slice of bread from his neighbor only to expire as he strained to swallow it. . . .

Still more died of thirst than of hunger. The prisoners' mouths were parched and cracked, and the Germans would pour in sewage water through the little window. The foul liquid would wet the prisoners' clothes, and they would strive to lick their neighbors' garments, fighting over the right to do so. . . .

Pinchas'l was hanging in midair. He could stand on his own two feet, yet he wouldn't lean on weaker men. His hands rose up in a silent prayer. His fingers clung to the bars on the small window. He remained suspended like this all night and awaited his end. And then the miracle happened. At dawn a clear, cool liquid dripped onto his shaking fingers. It was dew, dripping down from the top of the boxcar. . . .

In the morning Bogush remembered his friend Pinchas'l. All night Bogush had slept stretched out on the bed of corpses. He graciously offered his bed to Pinchas'l.

"Panzer Faust!" he reminded him.

Pinchas'l, who had just licked the dew off his fingers, tasting manna from heaven, stretched up and said pleasantly,

"God willing!"

❂   ❂   ❂

On the thirteenth day of the journey the train stopped and the doors were flung open. A spark of hope was lit up—was the journey at an end? No! The order was given to separate the dead from the living; to count the corpses and throw them outside. The train guard was given a rule of thumb: Anyone who walked out of the boxcar was alive; anyone who stayed inside was dead.

Pinchas'l was too weak to stand on his feet. He crawled out on all fours. He was not the only one who crawled. The train stood in a forest which was turning green. Inside the forest they unloaded the dead weight and began to dig a common grave for all those who had reached journey's end. Pinchas'l crawled along with all the other crawlers. The forest winds revived him, awakening in him a desire to eat and drink. The men around him began to chew the grass, smacking their lips, swallowing . . . what a delicacy! Not so Pinchas'l. His mind was lucid. He controlled himself. Something told him the grass was poisonous. Another human need was awakened in him. During the thirteen days of the trip he had controlled himself and did not relieve his body, out of shame, out of respect for man who was created in the divine image. Now he had his chance. . . . It was not easy. He lost a great deal of blood. But his body was cleansed.

The journey was resumed. The few who were strong enough to enter the clean boxcars went in. Among them was Pinchas'l. There was now enough room in the boxcar to walk around. . . . Because his body was clean and because he sat in a clean place he felt an urge to pray, to put on tefillin. From the days of his interment in Buchewald he had saved a solitary head tefillin, with torn straps. All during the journey he had not been able to use it because of the filth. Now his chance had come. He prayed with great feeling, with supreme fervor. He prayed without words. He had no strength to utter the words, nor did he remember exactly what to say. His was a prayer of the heart. His lips moved, his heart skipped, he prayed wordlessly, inarticulately.

When Bogush saw Pinchas'l pray, he was greatly moved. He clenched his fist as if to say,

"Panzer Faust!"

With this gesture Bogush was admitting that Pinchas'l faith was as strong as a fist. . . .

When Pinchas'l finished praying Bogush offered him a handful of sugar powder, which he, Bogush, had stolen from the supply car. Pinchas'l licked the sugar and his heart began to beat again. His blood began to run, his limbs responded to his will. A new hope bloomed in his heart.

"God willing!"

❈   ❈   ❈

By the nineteenth day Pinchas'l's hope that the journey will some day come to an end was beginning to dwindle. His faith was weakening. He felt as if the death train was destined to run on forever. At the same time he felt that his own end was approaching, quickly and inexorably. He took his pulse which began to falter: Fifty, forty. . . . It would soon stop. . . . His eyes were bulging out of their sockets. His stomach began to turn. . . . The last knell was about to be heard. . . .

Sinking, Pinchas'l was looking for a life line, something to hold on to. Countless times he had decided what to think of and what to do in his last moments, and now that the time came his train of thought was cut off. He knew he had to make his confession, but he did not remember what to say. How to confess. . . . Everything was forgotten, even those prayers he used to know by heart. He began to dream again. And what a clear and lucid dream it was!

His mother was standing beside him, holding his hand and leading him into a cave lit up with a magic light. When they entered the cave his mother proceeded to kindle the Sabbath lights. She covered her glowing face with the palms of her hands and began to whisper the blessing. At that moment a wonderful melody began to well up inside of him, the tune of *mizmor shir leyom hashabbat.* A song, a hymn for the Sabbath. Slowly the words rose up in his memory and joined the tune, the words and the tune welding together, "A boorish man will not know this, and a fool will not comprehend, that when the wicked flourish like grass and all the doers of iniquity sprout forth, it is that they may perish forever, but you, Lord, are forever exalted . . ." Wherefrom does Pinchas'l get the strength to open his mouth and sing such a mighty hymn? Is it only a dream, a vain imagining? . . .

Behind Pinchas'l's bent back stood Bogush whose voice cut into the dream.

"Nice time you've picked for singing. Why don't you open your eyes and see the fear of death which has overtaken the Germans. Hold out, Jew, hold out. Don't die on the verge of victory! Look outside and see all the forsaken tanks, the bombed out trains, the burning train stations, the multitudes of murderers down on their knees pleading for mercy . . ."

Pinchas'l woke with a start. The dream world vanished. Too bad! Too bad! On his chapped and shrivelled lips he still felt the sweetness of the words, healing and comforting: "When the wicked flourish like grass, and the doers of iniquity sprout forth, it is that they may perish forever, forever, forever . . ."

Pinchas'l opened his eyes and saw Bogush's flushed face and shining eyes. He understood at once what that outburst of joy meant, and again he tasted the reviving taste of the verse which rose out of his dream, "So that they may perish forever!"

Bracing himself, Pinchas'l whispered between his clenched teeth, "Panzer Faust?"

Bogush, scared and elated, let himself go and shouted,

"*Chvala Boska!* (Praise God!) I am also a believer son of believers! I am a Christian! My real name is Boguslav, which means, Praise God! But right now, on this great moment, I am scared to death. My crime follows me! I am afraid I will not live to see the day of victory! . . ."

144

It was not long before the train stopped in a small unknown station. There was great commotion, noise and confusion, and the sound of shooting and shouting: Out! Out!

The sealed doors of the boxcars were opened. There was no crowding at the exit, no pushing and shoving. Here and there someone barely got up from among the heaps of corpses. What was the number of those who had squeezed into the boxcar nineteen days earlier? Pinchas'l remembered the exact number. One hundred and thirty-six! Now only twenty-seven came out!

Pinchas'l spoke the number out loud—twenty-seven! Yes, twenty-seven, and he . . . was one of them. Bogush was another one.

Pinchas'l strained all his senses to understand what was going on, when he heard a screaming voice,

"*Achtung!* Listen! You have arrived at the great concentration camp of Mauthausen! This is train station Grossen A. From here to the camp you have to run by foot! The cabins are up on the hill. *Achtung!* Listen! There is no room here for Mussulmans (a Nazi expression for exhausted prisoners)! Those who fall behind will be shot! March! Forward!"

Forward? To run uphill? To run after nineteen days of torture in the death train?

Pinchas'l listened but did not grasp. He began to hear shots ringing out, coming from close range. He heard them and knew what they meant. He began to run, but he did not run, he flew. He flew effortlessly. What made him fly up the hill? Mother! She smiled at him with her beaming face like she did then, in the cave, during the lighting of the candles. And father? He heard his voice too. "God willing, God willing . . ."

"*Psha kreff!* (Dogs' blood!)" Pinchas'l heard a scream. He recognized Bogush's voice. He always said that curse. . . .

A shot, and then silence. Bogush stumbled, he fell down, cursing.

Pinchas'l continued to run. What made him run? The shooting? No. His mother's blessing, his father's prayer. . . .

"*Halt!* Stop! Here is Mauthausen! Mauthauzzzzzzen!"

Pinchas'l stopped running and stood still. In his ears echoed the satanic scream: Mauthauzzzzzzen!

But Pinchas'l stretched up, looked up to heaven and smiled, "God willing."

27

THE DANCE IN THE SHADOW
OF THE GAS CHAMBER

IN the liberated concentration camp of Bergen Belsen, among the brands saved from the fire of the crematorium, where each survivor could tell a thousand stories of miraculous events which happened to him, everyone pointed with great amazement to a strange and mysterious character.

"Here he is, *Das tanzendike hosid'l* (the dancing hasid)!"

I looked at the man they had pointed out, and my amazement was greater than theirs.

"Is this really the man whom you call 'the dancing hasid'?"

The figure before me was gaunt and bent, his face long and morose, his eyes dull, his beard and earlocks sparse, his body emaciated, shrivelled up, withdrawn. In short, he was the picture of sadness and desolation.

"What kind of a joke is this?" I asked in surprise. "Is it fair to poke fun at such an unfortunate person?"

"It's the truth! He *is* the dancing hasid! With his dancing he stopped the ovens in Auschwitz! You should really try to get him to tell you how he started dancing at the gate of the crematorium and how the Nazi commander, the head of the extermination operations, refused to put him into the oven. He pleaded with the German not to separate him from the rest of the Jews and he even tried to jump into the fiery furnace, but the chief murderer would not hear of it, no way!"

"If that is the case, why does he look so desolate, so totally disconsolate?"

"That's just the point! He is desolate because he has remained alive against his own wishes; because he owes his life to the chief murderer."

I tried to observe the "dancing hasid." I tried to fathom the mystery of his desolation. I tried to gain his confidence and get him to talk. I realized how the slightest mention of the dance made him shiver. But I wouldn't give up. Something told me that the mystery of the "dancing hasid" was also the mystery of many others, who like him jumped into the fiery furnace with a holy fervor, but whose sacrifice was accepted.

I couldn't get him to talk about the dance. This exalted experience was hidden in the depths of his soul, and any attempt to bring it out was an act of sacrilege. Nevertheless, I was able to gather bits of conversation, hints of memories, and some scattered facts, and put together this miraculous story about one of the junior hasids in the ghettoes of Poland. . . .

❀　　❀　　❀

"Dancing hasid, please tell me, what prompted you to dance in the desolation of the ghetto?"

"Not everyone succumbed to the gloom of the ghetto. A fighting underground arose in its midst, an underground of young hasidim who fought Satan with an ancient weapon—a rebellion against wickedness, a refusal to recognize the victories of tyranny. Those were rebels for the sake of heaven. Those young hasidim, whose Torah and whose faith was the whole essence of their being, created the resistence movement, which would not recognize any of the enemy's decrees. The enemy ordered every Jew from the age of twelve and up to do forced labor, and whoever did not have a work card would not get his meager ration of bread. The young hasidim formed a rebellious commune and went underground. They did not show up to do forced labor, and they used their own wits to find food. When hunger overcame them, some of them left their hiding place and they did go to do the forced labor, but they shared their bread with those who remained in hiding, to keep the flame of the Torah from going out, and to keep the hasidic fervor from dying."

"Do tell me, dancing hasid, did your dance continue even then, in the dying ghetto?"

"All that the enemy did in the ghetto was designed to break the will of the Jews. The Jewish badge, which we were ordered to wear on our clothes, was called by the enemy "a sign of shame." But they were grossly mistaken. Quite to the contrary. We were proud of it. To carry a yellow star of David which testified that one was Jewish—what could be better! Certain commandments in the Bible were meant specifically to single out the Jew. Mezuzah, tefillin, tzitzit, and growing beard and earlocks, what is their purpose? And Jewish clothes are certainly unmistakable. And so the junior hasidim who resisted all the decrees of the enemy accepted the yellow star as a commandment which the time had brought about. They kept that commandment and made sure that the yellow patch was neat and aesthetic, to enhance the commandment. And when they put it on for the first time they danced for joy and sang, "How happy we are, how fortunate we are . . ."

"Dancing hasid, please tell me, did you keep dancing till the last moment?"

"When things in the ghetto got too hopeless, the Jews began to understand that their chief concern now was how to die rather than how to live. The young hasidim in the underground did not forget for a moment that whatever they were doing was for the sole purpose of dying as Jews. An old hasid, a man of great learning, joined the young men and taught them the laws of martyrdom. He explained that in time of peace soldiers learn how to fight, but in times of war, when the trained soldiers are on the battlefield, they learn how to die honorably, how to keep their flag, and how to die for it if need be. This is how they were taught. They all pledged not to succumb to weakness, not to be seduced by the laughter of the devil, not to betray at the last moment, Heaven forbid, all that they had achieved while living in the ghetto.

"Dancing hasid, please don't evade me; tell me, did you keep the pledge?"

The dancing hasid was quiet. His desolate eyes scolded me. I felt as if I carelessly touched a holy string in the depths of his soul. And what the hasid failed to tell me, the people around him told me, and here is the short of it, the stuff from which the legend was spun with great reverence.

A band of young hasidim who rebelled and hid in the Lodz Ghetto and kept observing the laws of Judaism without any change, was captured during the liquidation of the ghetto. These young rebels were sent directly with the remnants of the people in the ghetto to Auschwitz. All during the trip to the camp the hasidim kept singing with a voice not theirs, with a supreme power. They entered the camp singing. They were led to the ovens singing. When they saw before them the chimneys of the crematorium they were seized with a holy fervor of the sanctifiers of the Holy Name of all time. In their ecstasy they clung to one another and formed a circle and started dancing, dancing and singing, "How happy are we, how fortunate are we, how happy . . ."

The chief executioner, the overseer of the ovens, who had seen a great deal in the course of his work of exterminating Jews, was startled to see the happy, dancing band.

"What is this? What kind of dancing is this?" he cried out in consternation.

"Those youngsters are hasidim!" one of the Jewish slaves who worked at the ovens explained. "They are full of faith, and they believe that the highest thing a Jew can achieve is to be burned as a Jew while hallowing God's name."

"I won't kill them! I won't help them fulfill their wish!" the head of the murderers decided summarily.

A strange conflict ensued.

The dancing hasidim, whose longing and devotion consumed their soul, started begging,

"We want to go in! We want to join the rest of the Jews! How happy are we, how fortunate are we!"

And the emissary of the devil, frightened and enraged, yelled out,

"No! You, I won't burn! It's out of the question!"

And then the dance died. The singing stopped. The close knit band fell apart, its joy turned into mourning, like someone who suddenly fell from the pure heavens to a dark abyss. Their sacrifice was not accepted. They were thrown back into grim reality. Most of them later on found their way to the ovens, like the rest of their Jewish brothers. The only one who survived was this one, known as the "dancing hasid."

"Dancing hasid, I won't ask you any more about your silence and your sadness! You have reached the highest rung of spiritual courage. What more is left for you to attain?"

28

MY NAME IS HAIM!

YOU ask me who I am? Don't you recognize me? They all recognized me immediately, everywhere I went. All of them, the hunters on all the roads, the pursuers on all the highways, the guards on all the borders. They all recognized me, summer and winter, in rain and snow, at dawn and in the dead of night. They all recognized me from afar, they smelled my odor. . . . And you still ask me who I am? Yes! I am a Jewish child! A Jewish child who climbs over every wall and jumps every partition. A Jewish child, who mocks all the pursuers and oppressors. A Jewish child who does not know the meaning of fear. I am a Jewish child!

Where did I come from? Why did I run? How did I escape? Why do you ask? You too have come to investigate me? Okay, I'll tell you my secret. I have come out of the pit of death. I have come out of an open grave! There I was born! Yes, believe me, there I was born all over again. Whatever happened before that I no longer remember, and if I do remember, I won't tell you. I won't tell you about my little sister and my two older brothers and the little baby, Uri, oh, that little one, small as a chick, and about Mother, who was taken away with all the children, except for me. . . . I won't tell you! No, I don't know anything! I was born in the pit. I was dead. I lay in the pit with the rest of the Jews, with children, many children, and I also yelled *Shema Yisrael*. I yelled *Echad* with all my might, until I was dead like the rest of

150

the dead. Later on I was quiet and I did not scream any more. Father held me all the time in his arms—like this, on the way to the forest he held me, and when we fell among the dead he held me—and I was dead already, and Father continued to hold me and squeeze me. . . . Yes, Father squeezed me, and it hurt, boy, did it hurt, and I was dead already, and the pain was terrible. And I forgot that I was dead already, and I began to scream. Everything was quiet all around, everyone in the pit was quiet, and I screamed, "Father!" And Father held my hands, and it really hurt. And I wanted to take my hand out, but Father would not let me. I yelled, but Father did not answer, because Father was dead. I yelled at the top of my lungs, and Father woke up. He did not yell, he only sighed. He asked quietly, "Ah, what is this?" And I asked, "Father, am I dead or alive?" And Father answered quietly, "Ah, my child, you are alive." And he asked me, "What's hurting you, son? Why are you crying?" I pulled my hand from under father's arm and I said, "It's all right, Father, it's not hurting any more." And Father whispered to me, "Be quiet, my son, all the Jews are dead, and I am dying too." So I yelled, "Father, I am not dead, I am alive." And Father whispered to me, "Lie down, my son, pretty soon they will fill up the pit with dirt and we will lie here with the rest of the Jews." I yelled, "Father, I am alive and I want to live. Come, Father, let's run away!" But Father did not want to leave the pit of the dead. It was hard for him to move, he was bleeding a great deal. And I clung to him. The blood made me cling to him, but I didn't want to lie down. He said to me, "Go out, my son, get out of the pit. I am dead. I am losing all my blood. But you are alive, and you want to live. You will come back to life out of the death pit, and your name will be Haim, life. With God's help you may reach the land of the living. Run, Haim, my son. Run fast. And live!"

Don't ask me any more questions. What more is there to know? I have told you everything. I ran away from the open grave to the nearby forest, and the trees of the forest became my friends, my brothers and companions. The trees let me climb on them and they hid me among their branches. And the weeds of the forest became my bed and my food. I whispered my secret to the things that grew in the forest, who I was and what my name was. But the hunters were after me; they surrounded the forest, and they nearly trapped me. Finally I came out of the forest. The enemy kept chasing me.

Entire armies after one child. They were armed from head to toe and they stood guard day and night, in every city, in the fields and in the villages, in the streets and on the highways, waiting to get me. I saw this and I understood that I was carrying a treasure, the most precious treasure in the world, worth all their effort and hard work to get their hands on it. From them, from the hunters, I learned how to guard that treasure. More than once did I lose my desire to live. And often I would start thinking of all the Jews who had remained in the pit, of my father and my mother and all the children. It occurred to me it was not right of me to leave them, for I was a Jewish child all alone, and what business did I have living among so many enemies? But whenever I saw that they were looking for another Jew and yet another Jew—I understood that a living Jewish child was the greatest treasure in the world, and I swore to guard that treasure, come what may! A few times they thought they had captured that treasure. They surrounded the houses and barricaded the streets and climbed on the rooftops and went down into the basements and searched everywhere. They had special instruments for detecting every little sound. I held my breath, and I repeated the oath in my mind, "My name is Haim, and I am going to live!"

Don't ask me when the chase ended. It did not end. The hunters changed their faces and their uniforms, but the chase went on. I heard people say, "The War is over!" and I heard bells ringing, "Victory has arrived!" and I heard singing and rejoicing in the streets, "Down with the enemy, all men are free!" I wanted to go outside and shout, "I am a Jewish child!" and I almost got trapped. The hunters had changed their uniform and were speaking a different language, but the chase was still on. A living Jewish child had remained the same treasure it was before, only now it had to be guarded even more closely, with greater secrecy and care. Again I escaped and crossed borders. On the borders there were other soldiers, soldiers who liked to play with children, soldiers who smiled. At first they smiled and played with me. They put me on their knees and gave me candy, and they proceeded to investigate me. "Where is your father and mother, son?" I wouldn't tell them. What should I tell them, that Father and Mother and all the children had remained there, in the pit, and that I alone have escaped from the pit? I kept quiet and I wouldn't tell them a thing. They asked me further, "And where do you live, son? Why are you running away? And where are you going?" I could no longer remain silent. I told them, "Where is there a place for me to live? You tell me. They chase me everywhere." I told them I used to live in the forest, where every bird has a nest, every animal a hiding place, every worm a place to sleep. I told them I was hiding in holes in the ground, in basements and in caves and I saw that every rat had a hole. And that the rats attacked me, because they were afraid I was going to steal their hole. And I didn't know where my hole was, and now they asked me where I lived. They continued to question me, "Are you a Jewish child?" and those who smiled stopped smiling. "What? Are there still Jewish children left in the world?" And the guards would refuse to let me cross the border, and I would sneer at all the guards and at all the borders. "My name is Haim, and I have arisen from the dead!"

What was the end? Don't ask. The hunters lay in wait for me everywhere, but me, Haim, they could not fool. I could recognize them from far away, and I also learned how to identify Jews. I could single them out among thousands of gentiles. . . . A Jew could hide all he wanted, he could speak any language and dress any way he chose, and I would still recognize him. How? Don't ask me. I won't tell you. And even if I did, you wouldn't understand. The Jew has two eyes . . . how shall I explain it? In one eye there is death, in the other eye life. One eye sees the pit of the dead and the river of blood and all that . . . and the other eye . . . I don't know how to say it. No, each eye has both life and death in it, and the eyes scream, and they stab, and they burn, and they are good, and they tremble, and they are so deep, those eyes. . . . You won't understand this. You weren't there. Me they can't fool any more. I saw one man dressed in a beautiful new uniform, a hunter like all the other hunters. I looked into his eyes, and I didn't ask him anything. He didn't ask me anything either, he didn't get a chance. I said to him right away, "Hear O Israel! My name is Haim!" And he clutched my hands and held me tightly the way my father had held me in the pit. He squeezed me in his arms, the way Father squeezed me in the grave, but it didn't hurt, and I didn't cry. And before I had a chance to say anything he knew everything. Everything. He said to me, "What a beautiful name—Haim! Ah, every Jew who is still living is given the name Haim, life! And you will

153

live with all the living Jews!" And he clutched me in his arms and said to me, "And I want you to know, that the Jews now have their own land, and that this land is like a mother for every Jewish child who has no mother, this land is the mother of all the Jews, and you will live there too!"

How did he bring me here? Don't ask me. It's a secret. I am not a child. Don't think I am still a child. I am not. . . . He squeezed me the way Father did and I didn't cry. He was good to me like a father and like a mother and I didn't cry. He carried me on land and on sea, and I didn't cry. The sea was good at first, but then it got bad. It raged and foamed and did unpleasant things, and I thought the sea had become like the death pit and was going to swallow up all the Jews, but I didn't cry. The sea screamed day and night and never stopped, and I told the sea, "My name is Haim, and I am going to live!" And the sea made peace with me, and the sea sang me a song like my mother once sang to our little baby. Ah, that baby, so little and so pretty, and mother rocked the baby, in her arms. . . .

No, I won't tell you any more. . . . And suddenly he woke me up and called out, "Haim, Haim!" He was carrying me on his shoulders. He was standing in the sea, knee deep in water, and I, my shoes and my feet were in the water. And he was carrying me, and I did not cry. He was coming out of the water, and everywhere I saw sand. Such pure sand! Only sand and more sand. He fell on the sand and he threw me down and he started to cry like a child. He said, "Haim, Oh, Haim, here you will live with all the Jews. Am Yisrael Chai!" And he scooped up handfuls of sand and played like a little child. And I lay on the sand, and the sand was hot and dry and soft, and the sand warmed me up like a mother, and I too began to cry . . . I cried only once. Don't ask me. I'll never cry again. I swore by my life and by my name Haim I would never cry again. I will only rejoice and sing and call out, "My name is Haim, and I want to live!" And my father, in the death pit, had promised me I was certain to go on living! And all the Jews along with the children who had fallen into the pit saying *Shema Israel*, all of them, all of them call out to me, Live, please live for our sake! And so, in spite of or because of all our enemies, I will pray, and I will shout, "Father, who lives in heaven, let me live for my father's sake, and for the sake of all the Jews, for my name is Haim!"